Sunset Ideas for
REMODELING YOUR HOME

By the Editors of Sunset Books and Sunset Magazine

Lane Books · Menlo Park, California

Edited by Sherry Gellner

*ON THE COVER: To take full advantage of a eucalyptus grove,
F. Malcolm George, Architect, opened the roof as well as the wall in his own home.
Photograph by Morley Baer.*

Executive Editor, Sunset Books: David E. Clark

Seventh Printing May 1973

Contents

THE FIRST STEP

As each remodeling project is unique, there can be no hard-and-fast rules to govern the remodeler. However, many of the problems you might encounter in remodeling can be precluded if you follow the general plan outlined in this book.

If you have seriously decided on a remodeling project, whether it is the simple removal of a partition or a more complex undertaking that will double the size of your existing house, you should consider these fundamental steps:

Consolidate Your Ideas. The entire family should confer on the remodeling project, making notes as to the desired end results. Discard any ideas that are obviously not feasible and discuss in detail those that seem most likely to help you obtain your goal. Next, outline the steps and factors involved in your project. If possible, make rough sketches of the proposed changes to the house. Be sure to take all measurements of the section of the house involved and to note pipe, electrical, and gas lines that might be involved.

Check Local Building Ordinances. It is a good idea to obtain a copy of your local building codes. These codes set construction standards for concrete, masonry, and carpentry work, cover zoning restrictions, and regulate standards for plumbing, heating, and wiring. Building restrictions and regulations often seem harsh and frustrating to the would-be remodeler, but they are based on practical considerations. Rules insure sound construction and safe, healthful homes.

Arrange for an Initial Consultation. With your basic idea in mind and your rough sketch, contact an architect, engineer, or new-home builder. They will be willing to review your situation for an equitable fee. Or you could check with your local building inspector, who in the long run, must approve your remodel plans.

These people can tell you what utility lines, bearing walls, or other obstacles might stand in your way.

IN REMODELING...

They can tell if your plan has closed the kitchen off from natural light, or if your deck/patio would be completely exposed to harsh prevailing winds. Perhaps you have neglected to allow adequate space for storage, or have devised an unworkable traffic pattern.

There are many factors to be taken into consideration, and this initial consultation might be just the step which could save you much money and many headaches.

Have Preliminary Plans Drawn. After your local building department has given preliminary approval to your rough draft, it is time to have a set of professional plans drawn up. This can be done by a draftsman, a designer, or an architect. Their services vary, and you should understand the differences between them.

A *draftsman* is a member of a skilled trade prepared to draw plans exactly per your instructions. If you are well acquainted with the building industry, and know which electrical conduits to specify, specific requirements for joists and studding, the pros and cons of various fixtures, you would be dollars ahead to secure the services of a competent draftsman for a modest hourly rate.

A *building designer* is a relatively new profession with most of the members belonging to the American Institute of Building Designers. The experienced designer will provide you with a preliminary drawing for a minor fee and a set of plans for a pre-arranged price. The designer will make constructive suggestions concerning your plan, and will help smooth out some rough edges.

An *architect* will draw up clearly specified plans and will even deal with the contractor himself. He will generally make all minor decisions himself, such as types of wire and size of joists, but he will consult you on any major changes. You also have the option of seeking the services of the architect for the plans only, and then working with the contractor yourself.

Unless they are retained on a consultation basis specifying an hourly fee, architects generally work on a flat percentage basis, in keeping with the total cost of the job.

Get Contractors' Estimates. Your next step is to contact at least two, and preferably three, contractors for a cost estimate of your remodeling project. There is no obligation of any kind or fee required on your part, and no firm commitment on theirs, but now you will have a good idea as to how your plans fit into the family budget.

If the cost is running higher than you had anticipated, this would be a good time for you to look into different materials available. Perhaps you can economize in areas not of primary concern.

Make Loan Arrangements. When applying for a bank loan, bring along your finished plans and the contractors' estimates. At this time you will also have to fill out an application for a Home Modernization Loan. The bank will then send to your home an appraiser, who will go over your existing structure, study your proposed additions and alterations, and recommend the amount allowable for a construction loan.

Although the bank is the logical source of home improvement loans, you may find it advisable to investigate other sources, such as borrowing against your life insurance policy or from a company credit union. Or, if you choose to use your savings account, you will find that most lending institutions have a procedure enabling you in effect to borrow your own money for a very low rate of interest.

Select a Contractor. You should keep in mind when selecting a contractor that the contractor with the lowest bid is not necessarily the one for you. You should base your decision on his reputation in home building—he should be cooperative, competent, and financially solvent. He is the one who will be hiring, supervising, and coordinating the work of the different building craftsmen, and he is the one who orders the materials.

When trying to choose a contractor, you can always contact homeowners for whom a contractor has previously worked. You can also check with your bank or local credit bureau for his financial reputation. Subcontractors and material suppliers can also be contacted for their opinions. The contractor himself should be willing to discuss his business practices with you.

When all major and minor decisions have been made concerning your plans, and when your loan arrangements have been made, the contractor can give you a firm bid. Then, arrangements can be made as to how the contractor will be paid. Usually payments are made either on the installment plan, voucher system, or in one lump sum upon completion.

The contractor then secures the building permit from the city or county.

FINANCING YOUR REMODELING PROJECT

Financing is a major factor in any remodeling project whether it is a major addition or a small alteration. The ideal way to finance a remodel is to anticipate the operation a few years in advance, open a special savings account, and deposit a given amount monthly. This allows you to begin your project when your target date arrives, and also eliminates interviews with loan officers and saves you a substantial amount of interest.

However, the average person wanting to remodel confers with the loan officer at his bank once he has a rough idea as to how involved his construction job will be. Although the lending institution will not be in a position to commit itself as to exact amount, terms, or interest rate until you have a completed set of plans and a concrete bid on the work, the loan officer can give you the bank's "rule of thumb" regulations governing modernization loans.

The bank will require of you a satisfactory financial statement. In addition, the current market value of your home and the amount of your equity will be taken into consideration. Normally ¾ of your equity is the maximum amount that they will lend. Most banks hold to a maximum of 5 years for this type of loan which has to be fully amortized (paid in equal monthly installments including both principal and interest with the last payment paying off the loan and all of the interest in full).

Smaller loans will often be held to a maximum of three years compared to five years for larger home improvement loans.

FHA, finance companies, and commercial and industrial loan companies usually offer home improvement loans. Each institution has its own rules governing the amount of loan, length of loan, and amount of interest charged.

Other Types of Financing. If you have paid off your present home mortgage, you might consider remortgaging your home. If you are still paying on your present home mortgage, you could refinance your house to get the money you need. Check with your home-mortgage-holder to see if you are eligible for an open-end mortgage, or if a second mortgage on your home would be practical.

If you have permanent life insurance, you can borrow against the cash value of your policy at a favorable rate of simple interest.

Each lending institution carries its own conditions on home improvement loans, so look into all phases of the loans which interest you before making your final decision.

REMODELING TIPS

• Have your property lines surveyed if you think your remodeling project might extend past your prescribed setback or encroach on your neighbor's property.

• Have preliminary soil tests made on the proposed site of your addition. Encountering solid bedrock could raise your construction costs, while unstable soil could cause serious settling problems.

• Order a structural pest control inspection if there is even a remote possibility of termites, fungus, dry rot or water damage in your existing structure.

• Provide for adequate fire escapes if your addition will turn your home into two stories. If it is not possible to have more than one stairway, be sure to provide for a fire escape from a large window or balcony.

• Anticipate heating requirements in advance. It might be more practical and more economical to install a new heater in your addition than to add vents to your regular heating unit.

• Study the exterior design of your existing structure and correlate your remodeling design with it.

• Allow for adequate natural light to remain in your existing structure. If your addition takes away some natural light, a skylight can be added to your existing structure.

• Plan your addition in detail, keeping in mind furniture arrangement and traffic patterns.

• Keep in mind your neighbors when planning your remodeling project. A second story addition might block a neighbor's view, or your altered drainage pattern might cause problems in the adjacent yard.

• Design bath or kitchen add-ons or remodels with existing plumbing hook-ups in mind.

GAINING LIVING SPACE
BY ADDING ON

Original house was pleasant but small and undistinguished before remodeling. By adding space above the carport the owners gained 800 square feet of living space. The photo below shows the completed addition. Cedar shingles and walnut-stained window frames and trim create handsome new exterior. (For more about the remodeling of this house, see page 28.)

They added on to both ends of little house

Rather than move to gain space for their growing family, the owners of the small two-story house shown at right enlisted the services of an architect to see what could be done by remodeling. His solution was to add a new living room at one end and a third bedroom and bath over the kitchen at the other end. Since there was a steep roof over the two-story portion of the existing house, a new roof was simply extended at the same height forward over the new sunken living room and back over the kitchen area.

Architect: James W. P. Olson.

Before. *The house was attractive, but too small.*

Roofline was extended *over addition which contains new living room; new chimney was also added.*

Brick steps lead *from new living room addition up to level of existing house; French doors open to entryway.*

Sleeping loft *in boy's new bedroom is like having a tree house indoors — for play, study, and sleep.*

Living room addition *is shaded area at left. Plan above shows addition of new bedroom, bath, and closet space created on the second level by raising the roof over the kitchen. Original stairway which led upstairs to playroom and bedroom was lengthened for convenient entrance to new bedroom.*

Front entrance *is through a small greenhouse into what is now the family room.*

Living space was more than doubled

The original house, a pleasant one-bedroom stucco structure, occupied a highly desirable view site at one end of a quiet lane, but its size (777 square feet) was totally inadequate for a couple with children. What happened was a kind of space explosion: The owners added 1,760 square feet of new living space, not including decks and carport. The expanded house still retains much of the effect of the original stucco house, although there is little left of the old shell.

Architects: A. Jane Duncombe, Donald James Clark, and Thomas Higley.

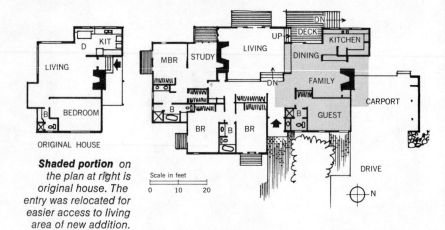

Shaded portion on the plan at right is original house. The entry was relocated for easier access to living area of new addition.

Expanded house is sited among large native oaks. Unless told, a first-time viewer would never suspect that 777 square feet of living space had been added. Exterior still retains feeling of original stucco house.

Steps lead down from deck (reached from dining or living room) to garden. Large windows open the view to spreading oaks and area beyond. Door directly under stairway leads to basement and storage area.

Original house had large living room windows facing the view, but no direct access to the garden.

Sunken living room is part of addition; has two sets of stairs leading up to level of the existing house, new bedroom area.

Box house was opened wide, doubled in size

Prior to remodeling, this house was a small rectangular box under a pitched roof with wide overhangs. In successive stages of remodeling, the box was gradually opened up to encompass additional floor space. The horizontal lines of the house were retained in each new addition, and the rooms were opened to the garden view.

A kitchen wall was pushed out to form an eating area, and the living room-dining room wall was moved out to the roof line to form a large glass-enclosed bay. There the roof's pitch necessitated a dropped ceiling. Sliding doors lead directly to the garden.

A separate room and bath were added at the living room end of the house, with a connecting hall and entryway. The glass-wall entryway, with its garden view, immediately suggests to visitors the pleasant indoor-outdoor relationship achieved in the rest of the house.

The slope of the lot allowed the owners to build a two-story bedroom wing at the other end of the house without raising the roof line. The master bedroom occupies the top floor; on the lower floor are a bedroom and bath. A stairway hall separates the area from the rest of the house and blocks some noise.

Architect: Burr Richards.

Entry approach from carport, driveway, and parking area. Patio area to right is set off by planting wall.

Living room-dining room wall was pushed out four feet and replaced with 4 by 6 post support, sliding glass doors.

Ceiling detail in living room extension. Skylight was cut in original roof overhang to provide additional daylight.

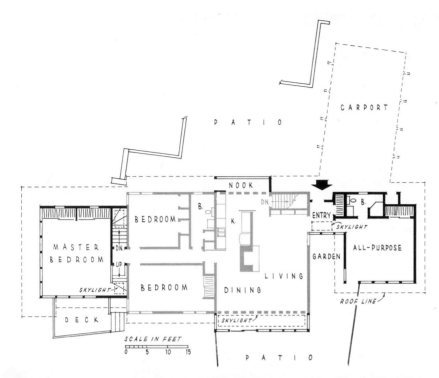

Shaded rectangle contained only 1,040 square feet of living space. Addition around this area increased the area to 2,100 square feet. Horizontal lines of house were retained and new rooms were opened to the view.

Long, low lines of house repeat the contours of the site. Remodeling was done in successive stages. Walls of original house were pulled out into alcoves and wings which were oriented toward the garden view.

An old cottage grew into a spacious new house

The house shown below was originally a small two-bedroom cottage. Located at the rear of a long and narrow lot, it was bounded at one end by a lane and at the opposite end by a street — but with the front of the cottage facing the lane.

To expand the house, the owners reversed the plan, orienting it towards the street, and doubled the floor space by adding on to what was originally the rear of the house. The original living room and dining room became bedrooms, the front porch became a master bath, and the kitchen became a breakfast room.

The new construction included a family room-dining room, living room, kitchen, and entry. Inside, old blends with new. The tobacco store cabinets in the kitchen were found in a secondhand store and stained to match the new green and white flooring.

After remodeling. *Carport is architecturally connected to the house by framework of a new deck off the living room.*

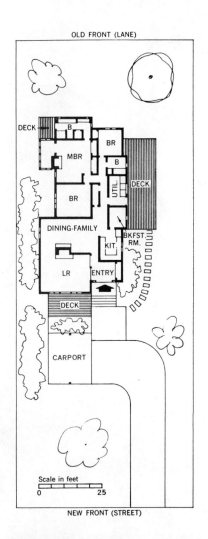

OLD FRONT (LANE)

DECK
B
MBR
BR
B
BR
UTIL.
DECK
DINING-FAMILY
BKFST. RM.
KIT.
LR
ENTRY
DECK
CARPORT

Scale in feet
0   25

NEW FRONT (STREET)

New kitchen is U-shaped, has storage cabinets that reach to the ceiling.

Before. New rooms were added to the front of a narrow lot.

Master bedroom with fireplace was old living room.

A house that grew as the family grew

By adding rooms around the periphery of their small house, the owners doubled its floor space and hardly interrupted the family routine during remodeling.

For space that had been carport and driveway, the architects designed a master bedroom and bath, a new utility room, and a large family room. The new carport, at the front of the house, provides parking places for two cars.

The new family room, comparable in size to the living-dining room, has a built-in home office behind double doors, storage space under the eating counter, window walls on two sides, and sliding doors opening to the terrace and to the back garden. A minimum amount of furniture keeps floor space free for children's play.

Architects: Bystrom and Greco.

Home office *is located in corner of new family room.*

Large, well lighted *family room has cantilevered eating counter connecting to a pass-through from the kitchen.*

Square footage of original kitchen remained the same, but equipment was updated, counters redone in laminated plastic. Sink and working surface command view of both family room and play area outside.

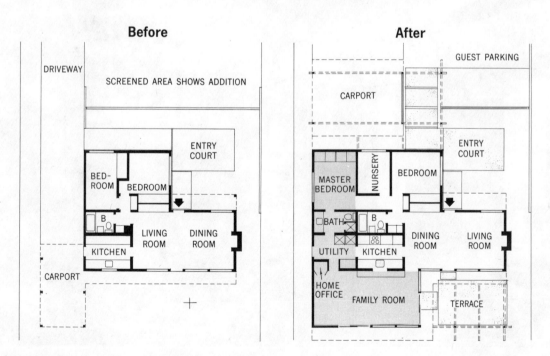

Before

After

Floor plans show how new rooms, terrace, and entry court were added on to the periphery of the original house.

They remodeled for space and spaciousness

It is often difficult to build an addition to a house on a hill sloping up from the street. But the architect solved this site problem — and the owners' need for more living space — neatly and dramatically by designing a new living room at a lower floor level than that of the existing house, while maintaining the roof line at the same level.

The result is a warm, spacious new room that uses its extra ceiling height to provide views of surrounding trees and of the sky. It cannot be called a glass-walled room, but windows and doors are large and take advantage of a foliage background.

The existing house received little structural alteration. The former living room became a family room-workroom. The kitchen was not moved but was redesigned to be more efficient and to open into a family dining area. The kitchen's former bay window became a vantage point open to the new living room below.

Architect: Raymond Kappe.

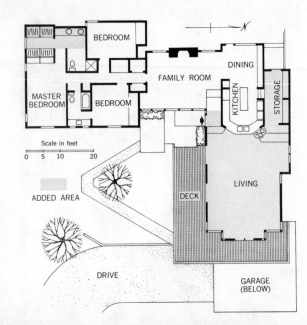

Kitchen overlooks living room, yet clutter is hidden. Natural light comes from the skylight and clerestory windows.

Night view shows lofty ceiling of the living room, its roof level with that of the original house.

Thirty-foot-long room, seen from kitchen, opens onto streetside deck, raised portion of the ceiling is wood to match the walls.

New deck extends around two sides of the added room and out over the garage. Front door is at far left of photo.

Once a terrace...now a dining room

When a corner of a house is knocked out to add interior space, something in its place is needed to hold up the roof. The architect solved the problem for this remodel by using a peeled cedar pole in the new room. Along with an overhead bay for direct lighting, the pole helps define an alcovelike space that has a pass-through formed by a section of new counter and a sliding caned panel.

Architect: Burr Richards.

Before room addition, *house had odd corners on this side.*

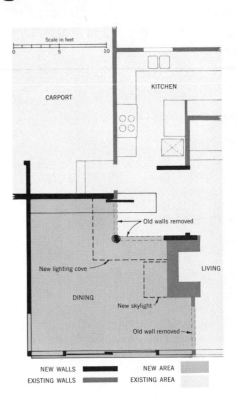

Scale in feet
0   5   10

CARPORT

KITCHEN

Old walls removed

New lighting cove

DINING

LIVING

New skylight

Old wall removed

| NEW WALLS | NEW AREA |
| EXISTING WALLS | EXISTING AREA |

New dining room *opens to the kitchen. Pole occupies the former exterior wall corner and supports the lighting cove.*

They added another living room

Adding a living room isn't a common way to remodel, but it makes good sense when the family needs more space and the existing living room can't be enlarged. The addition pictured below includes dining room and serving pantry; it left the former living room as a more intimate sitting room.

Architect: Arthur T. Brown.

New living room has one wall of glass which is shaded by a wide overhang and wing wall.

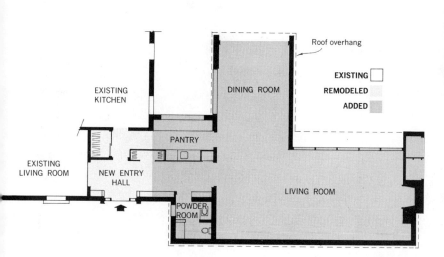

Floor plan. Remodeled entry and new pantry link new rooms to existing house.

The addition, at right, has a flat, low roof.

A new master bedroom—in the trees

Adding a bedroom to a house situated on a steep slope
with three stories on the downhill street side
and two in the rear presented a most unusual problem for
the designer.

With no room for expansion on level ground, the
only solution was to add to the house on the street side
at the main floor level, building the addition out
over the hill and supporting it on steel columns set
into the slope below.

Simple, spacious, and elegant, the addition
harmonizes with the existing stucco house and contributes
a new entry, a master bedroom with a deck among tree
branches, a new bathroom, and unusually generous closets.

Design: Craig Ellwood.

Shaded area shows addition; includes new entry, hallway, double-sinked bath, large bedroom with its own deck.

Bedroom is built on slender steel columns sunk deeply into sloping hillside; dense foliage covers supports.

New entry is near former entry at rear of house on downhill side. At left, addition has louvered window.

Master bedroom has mirrored closet doors reaching to the ceiling and reflecting the deck, trees across the room.

Entry hall leads to the new bedroom past wall of ceiling-height closets.

Bathroom, behind the mirrored wall (see photo above) has two entries.

Make-up mirror is lighted by 28 clear bulbs and from skylight above.

Sleeping loft for teen-age daughters

A new loft is the major acquisition in this spacious remodel. It contains bedroom, sitting area, and bath for two teen-age daughters. As shown in the sketch at right, parts of the existing roof were removed and replaced by a higher roof to make room for the loft. Openings in the loft overlooking the family room are not glassed in, while those above the enclosed patio are. The latter give a view of nearby mountains and let light into the loft through screened panels in the patio roof. Additional light comes through windows at one end of the loft and through a skylight in the sitting area.

Architect: Robert F. Gordon.

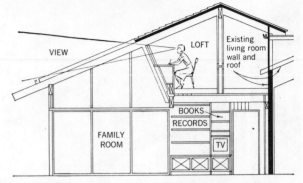

Cross section shows new loft above the existing dining room.

Partition and step *divide a long loft into bedroom and sitting areas. Truss construction suspends loft from the roof.*

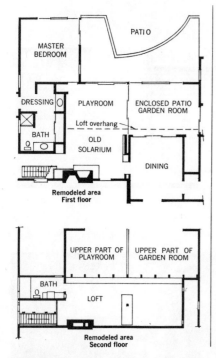

Old solarium *became new family room.*

Sliding door *to the family room disappears into wall slot shown at the left.*

Patio garden room *has open, screened panels in the roof to permit a view of mountains from loft windows opposite.*

They raised the roof to gain a bedroom wing

A teen-age girl has this bedroom-bath-dressing room suite all to herself — an exciting change from sharing a bedroom wing with three brothers.

A major remodeling project called for adding a family room to the main floor of the house. It was feasible at the same time to extend and raise the original roof to accommodate a second story suite. It consists of a large open bedroom flanked by a bathroom and a closet-dressing room.

The area can be isolated from the rest of the house by sliding shoji screens across the open sections of the balcony. With the screens open, the balcony is often used as a stage for puppet shows, with the sliding panel serving as curtains and the audience watching the action from below.

Architect: Joseph L. Williams.

Large window rising to roof peak plus smaller one opposite provide good daylight and cross-ventilation.

Original roof was raised for addition of girl's room.

Balcony bedroom is reached by flight of stairs from family room; can be closed off by sliding shoji screens.

Space was gained by adding a second story

By adding a second story over the garage, the owners gained a much needed bedroom-bath-sitting room complex. At the same time, remodeling of the lower floor produced a new dining room that is open to the garden and a completely updated kitchen. As shown in the floor plans below, part of the space formerly occupied by the two-car garage now houses the furnace and a separate pantry and utility area.

Architects: Rosekrans, Broder, and Siegel.

Second-level addition is compatible with the design of original house, uses former space above the garage and contains a new bedroom-bath-sitting room complex.

Sitting room, a quiet retreat for parents, is on front part of addition.

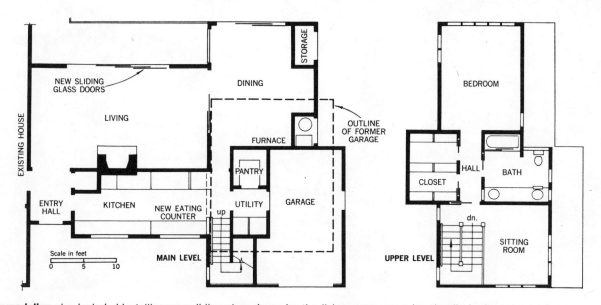

Remodeling also included installing new sliding glass doors for the living room, removing the tile in the entry, and refinishing the hardwood floor underneath. A louvered door closes off the kitchen from the utility and pantry area.

New bedrooms above...playroom, carport below

Adding living space above a garage or carport is rarely more successfully accomplished than it was here. The architect began with the small two-bedroom house pictured on page 7 and transformed it into what appears to be a new home.

The new two-story addition contains two bedrooms and bath upstairs; a carport and a playroom below. The original house's front entry was simplified, and a new doorway was cut into a bedroom (now a study) for direct access to the living room.

Matching windows, door frames, and interior trim and molding tie house and addition together. The entire exterior is finished with natural cedar shingles. Window frames and window walkways (for washing second-story windows) are stained dark walnut.

The existing carport and adjoining storage room were completely demolished before the addition was begun.

Architect: John Case Hansen.

Floor plans at right show how 800 square feet of living space were added to the original house. Exterior brick facing that decorated the front of the house was removed and used to raise the fireplace chimney 10 feet.

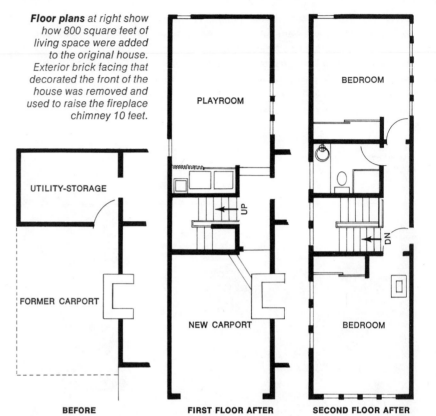

UTILITY-STORAGE

FORMER CARPORT

PLAYROOM

UP

NEW CARPORT

BEDROOM

DN

BEDROOM

BEFORE

FIRST FLOOR AFTER

SECOND FLOOR AFTER

Casement windows admit just as much light as before. Raised deck leads to entry.

Double doors open into new playroom situated behind carport. Projection of the addition into garden created a sunny outdoor annex to the playroom and kitchen.

New playroom has outside staircase

When this shingled house was built, the idea of a separate play and work room for children wasn't considered. So when the owners asked the architect to design a playroom addition, it posed a bit of a problem.

Like many other older homes built on a small lot, there was no room for expansion at the sides. There was room to build on toward the back of the lot, but a playroom added on to the dining room would not relate to the children's bedrooms and would, in fact, block the main access from house to garden—which is through the dining room to a floor-level porch.

The solution was to convert a second-story sundeck over the kitchen into the playroom and connect it to the garden and outdoor play area below by spiral stairs. The children enter their domain from their bedrooms and can pursue activities well away from main living areas. From the kitchen below, their mother can hear confrontations that get overly noisy and can watch comings and goings on the spiral stairs.

Architect: Sanford Pollack.

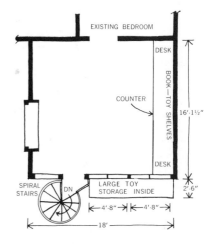

Built-in desk *at each end of counter has several storage drawers. Cavelike area under windows is for big toys. Ceiling is 12 feet high, has sky-turned windows.*

Staircase spirals *up to a new playroom, keeps traffic away from the work area.*

Traffic problem solved by new breakfast room

Adding a breakfast room solved a traffic problem for the owners of this remodel. The old breakfast room, whose space is now shared by a kitchen office and the expanded entry hall, was the main through route for kitchen, entry hall, and dining room.

The architects designed the addition to permit a rerouting of the traffic as well as to create the space for the office and a sewing alcove (not pictured). The kitchen itself was little changed, except for a new openness, new counters, and a new skylight.

Architects: Matlin & Dvoretzky.

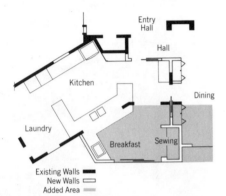

Existing Walls ▬
New Walls ▭
Added Area

Former kitchen window became wide opening to new room. The counter, 4 feet across, is all on one level for easy serving. Skylight was added to the kitchen.

New breakfast room has laminated plastic eating counter 36 inches high, gas-fired barbecue, room for table.

Kitchen office desk stands where entry to dining room was. Light is recessed under the shelf above.

REARRANGEMENT OF EXISTING SPACE

Former kitchen was spacious but antiquated. Sink-dishwasher unit was makeshift, windows were small. Behind the camera was a dark and inconvenient laundry room and back of that an unused maid's room, closet, and bath. By removing two walls (once located where front beams now show in photo below), the owners not only gained an up-dated kitchen, but a large and spacious family room. (For more details on this rearrangement of existing space, see page 36.)

Everything was changed...
from the street in and basement up

The "before" photograph shown at right doesn't begin to show the ramshackle condition of this house when the owners bought it. But its view location was excellent and the price seemed to make it a good investment.

With the help of the architect, a major remodeling project was launched in which just about everything was changed. Several weight-bearing beams were replaced. Most of the plumbing and wiring was also replaced. Among the most major improvements was the relocation of the entry and the stairs (see floor plans).

The kitchen was completely done over to provide more cabinets and counter space and a pass-through to the dining area.

Scarcely a window remains as it was. Windows that faced the street were removed or redesigned to provide more privacy; others were enlarged to take advantage of the view and admit more light.

The dark and unfinished basement was converted to a recreation room, bedroom, and bath. Oversized bricks were used for the recreation room floor. Hardwood, tile, or carpeting were used for floors elsewhere. Walls were finished both with plaster and with leftover pieces of hardwood flooring.

Architect: Robert Eyre.

Before: *House on corner lot had poorly placed doors and windows; inside, an awkward floor plan, unfinished basement.*

Fireplace was faced *with natural cedar strips. Window at the right marks the former front door location.*

New entry hall *provides abundant closet space behind the louvered doors at the right. Stairs at right lead to lower level.*

After. Wood deck from sidewalk leads to new front door, entry hall (former entrance was directly into living room).

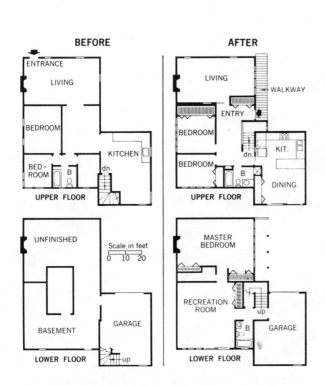

BEFORE

ENTRANCE

LIVING

BEDROOM

KITCHEN

BED-
ROOM   B   dn.

UPPER FLOOR

UNFINISHED

Scale in feet
0   10   20

BASEMENT   GARAGE

LOWER FLOOR   up

AFTER

LIVING

WALKWAY

ENTRY

BEDROOM

dn.   KIT.

BEDROOM   B

DINING

UPPER FLOOR

MASTER
BEDROOM

RECREATION
ROOM   up

B   GARAGE

LOWER FLOOR

Entry was moved to one side, eliminating the living room as a throughway. Note enlargement of upper floor bath.

New cabinets, built-ins, and lighting make kitchen a pleasant work area. Stove controls are above the hood.

A complete change-around

Most people wouldn't have considered this little house suitable for remodeling. Over the years since it was built as a summer cottage the elements had gradually weakened its structure until it was almost uninhabitable. The house was questionably supported by 4 by 4-inch joists spaced 3 feet apart and spanning over 12 feet.

The architect was well aware of the problems when he bought it, but was also certain that he could make it structurally sound and suitable to his family's needs. His first task was to jack up the house and pour a proper foundation. The floor plans show how he rearranged the existing space to change the house from a one-bedroom cottage to a three-bedroom, two-bath house with a generous studio.

Architect: Igor Sazevich.

Weathered old house sagged, barely hung together.

Remodeled house has two-level section added to front, with entry below, new bath above. No windows face street.

Living, dining rooms were enlarged by incorporating old glassed-in porch. Clerestory windows admit more light.

Former attic space now houses three bedrooms and bath; windows open to view.

FIRST FLOOR BEFORE

FIRST FLOOR AFTER

By removing two walls, they gained a family room

When they remodeled the kitchen in their old California-Monterey style house, the owners wanted to include a large family room. They also wanted to improve the lighting and incorporate new equipment and materials, yet keep the kitchen and family room in the same tradition as the rest of the house. (See page 31 for another view of how walls were removed to gain space.)

The working area in the new kitchen is clearly defined so a watchful eye can be kept on five small children. The dark oak cabinets and beams, the handcrafted tile counters, and the gray-green heavy-gauge linoleum floor retain the old California feeling.

Design: Janean.

Dotted lines indicate former walls. Sink, refrigerator and range, form conventional and workable triangle. Small sink eliminates some traffic.

Family room-kitchen was originally three rooms. Island with two sinks provides work and serving space near the table.

From three small rooms to one big room

After the children grow up, a family often has bedrooms it no longer needs, taking valuable floor space that could better serve some other use. In the house shown here, two adjoining unused bedrooms and a hall were simply eliminated, so the space could be converted to a dining-family room complex.

A pass-through was opened up from the kitchen to the new room for easy serving. Large doors in a new glass wall (not shown) open the room to a good-sized deck area and a rock garden beyond. A sloping hillside provides a natural barrier to the prevailing wind, making the deck an enjoyable place to relax a great part of the year.

Architect: Jerry Gropp.

Newly opened-up room reaches back toward the entry hall and living room beyond. Pass-through to kitchen is at left.

The old kitchen is now the family room

When the owners moved into this older house, they wanted to bring the kitchen up-to-date, yet retain its country quality. At the same time, they wanted a family room.

A review of the original floor plan quickly pointed out that the breakfast room, off by itself, occupied the choice corner position. The kitchen was in the traffic pattern, dark, and inefficient. And the only way to reach a basement wine cellar was by an outside stairway.

The designer's new plans called for locating the kitchen in the dead-end space where the breakfast room had been, relocating some doors to improve air circulation, bringing the outside staircase in under the laundry room, and adding storage space.

Design: Janean.

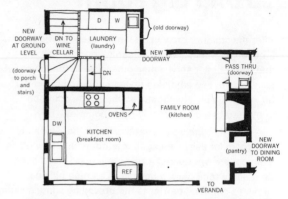

Plan shows former uses in parentheses. Kitchen is now separated from the family traffic pattern.

Family dines at oak table under an antique lamp. The fireplace is new. Dining room is seen beyond pass-through.

Laundry room *with well-organized storage now adjoins the family room instead of kitchen. New doorway is at right.*

Maple work counter *is at a low height (33 inches).*

Tile-lined alcove *includes cooktop, warming drawers below.*

One kitchen wasn't adequate, so they added another

This kitchen is really two. They work particularly well for a cook who specializes in exotic foods. Several kinds of dishes can be prepared for a dinner party without running out of room.

Even before moving into the house, the owners knew that the original kitchen wouldn't be adequate. So with the aid of an architect, they remodeled the existing breakfast area into a second cooking center.

The design was predicated on hiding a favorite range and at the same time giving maximum counter and storage space. A new bar counter doubles as a serving counter.

Architect: Donald James Clark.

Original kitchen *has new refreshment counter at left, new refrigeration units at right, and framed menus from around the world decorate the walls. New hardware and moldings unify it with the second kitchen.*

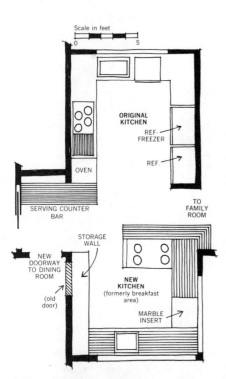

Former breakfast area *becomes the new kitchen. Counter has marble baking slab.*

Second kitchen *with original breakfast-area windows has a maple counter, new sink, and (behind counter in foreground) a favorite old range.*

Floor-to-ceiling cabinets *with Dutch doors provide generous dish storage next to range; shelves are adjustable.*

Baking equipment *is stored in large lazy Susan in a corner of the second kitchen; doors have magnetic catches.*

A new breakfast room, kitchen, sewing-room office

This remodel started out as a modest deck-and-stairway project to eliminate an inside stairway. As the work proceeded, more and more possibilities were seen, until the end result included a whole new kitchen wing with a breakfast room, and a combination sewing room and kitchen office.

The original kitchen was square and sacrificed some space to stairs leading down and outside; two of its major appliances were in direct line of traffic from hall to breakfast room. It is now a well planned corridor kitchen, opening at one end into a new breakfast room (enlarged to accommodate a family of six) and at the other, to the pleasant and much used sewing room-kitchen office. The 5½-foot-wide "corridor" permits limited foot traffic without inconveniences to the cook.

To lessen the number of steps between the cooktop and the sink, the architect moved the counter and lower cabinets along the inside wall toward the center of the room.

Architect: Charles D. Stickney.

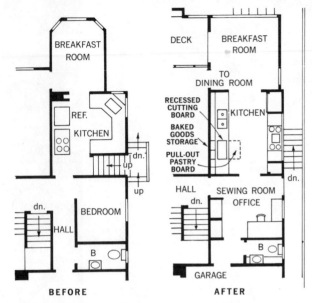

Plans show how interior stairway was replaced by exterior stairs to free floor space for new kitchen.

Tiled cooking alcove, flanked by refrigerator and double ovens, is generous in size and in storage space.

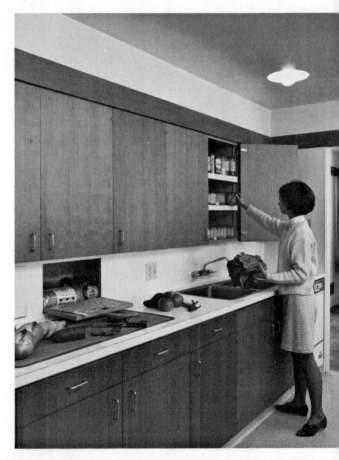

Opposite wall has long expanse of cabinets and counter. Cutting board is set flush in laminated plastic counter.

Sewing room-office combination was a former bedroom. Low table holds sewing machine or typewriter.

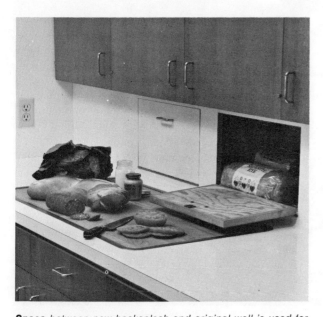

Space between new backsplash and original wall is used for tin-lined compartments to keep food fresh.

Pull-out board below drawers and behind cabinet door provides extra work space for baking, food preparation.

This kitchen is all in one wall

With 14 feet of hardwood counter between the wall ovens and the refrigerator, this remodeled kitchen doesn't conform to the compact working triangle usually considered ideal. Yet the owner found that it works beautifully.

Before the remodeling, the kitchen was 12 feet square and shared the remainder of its present space with a screened porch. The screened porch was eliminated, along with some doors that routed too much traffic through the kitchen; these two areas were made into one large room with windows on three sides. Two of the windows now function as pass-throughs to a new deck.

The table in the center of the room provides a central working space that would otherwise be missing. Besides serving as a barrier to keep spectators out of the way, it serves all the needs of kitchen counter space—it's a resting spot for groceries on their way to the food pantry, a work table for both the cook and small children, a family dining table, and on occasion a place for informal dinners.

The floor is red tile with a lacy Madeira rug under the table. The cabinets are pressed wood with a clear sealer. Everyday dishes and glasses are stored directly above the dishwasher. Four recessed ceiling lights illuminate the counter.

Architects: Beebe-Hersey.

BEFORE

AFTER

Complete kitchen *built in along one wall has double oven, gas cooktop, stainless steel sink, dishwasher, and refrigerator. Open shelves above store dishes, stretch across windows but do not cut out needed light.*

Their new bath was the old front porch

In remodeling, the owners reversed the floor plan, so that the house faced the main street, and made a master bedroom and bath out of the living room and front porch.

The generous floor space in the 7½ by 13-foot porch made it possible to include a large linen closet and a built-in sun lamp couch — a pleasant idea for the winter months. Along the wall opposite the couch is a compartmented shower stall and alongside the linen closet, an enclosed toilet.

The handsomely appointed lavatory opens directly off the bedroom through the original front door. Two rows of blue and yellow tile form a backsplash around the lavatory counter.

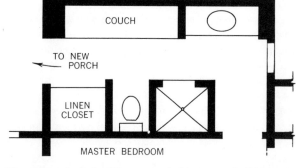

Plan shows bath facilities separated from sun-bathing area.

Sun-bathing couch in its own alcove has three wall-mounted sun lamps which are connected to a timer also on the wall.

Front porch became new master bath. The front door was retained but the windows were sealed, new porch was added.

Lavatory opens (through original front door) off the master bedroom, has a Mexican tiled backsplash and red floor tiles.

Two can use this roomy new bathroom

Two things definitely needed to be replaced in this house: the tub in this bathroom and the furnace, located in a room alongside the bath. Moreover, the 17-year-old bathroom was showing its age; and it was inefficient in that it was used mainly by two young daughters who often wanted it at the same time. Since the furnace room alongside had considerable unused floor space, the owner decided to undertake a complete remodeling of the bathroom while replacing the tub and furnace.

The designer relocated the furnace (this cost little extra since the old unit was being replaced). He gave it a convenient access door on the exterior of the house and moved the wall separating it from the bathroom.

With the floor space gain, and by moving the toilet next to the new bathtub, he was able to transform the drab room into a handsome, two-compartment bathroom with two access doors to the hallway and a sliding pocket door between compartments. There are two lavatories for the girls, ample storage cabinets underneath the counter, and a large linen closet on the wall alongside.

Design: Tom Sanford.

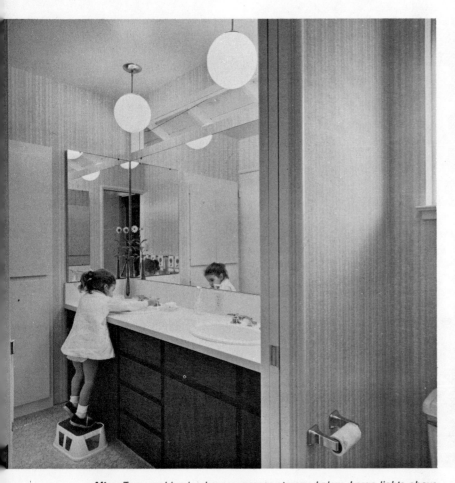

After. Two washbasins have generous storage below. Large lights above and generous-sized mirrors make room seem spacious.

Before. Bathroom accommodated only one person; furnace alongside had considerable unused space.

Separate compartment houses new tub and toilet, can be closed off by a sliding pocket door.

IDEAS FOR EXTERIOR FACE LIFTING

Old front door opened off screened-in porch on upper level. New stairway, located in space occupied by porch, leads from new entry on lower level to upper living areas. Horizontal lines of house were emphasized by extension of eave line below upper floor and by new covered entry. Bay windows replaced original windows in living room at right to bring in more light, open up view into the trees. (For more details on this remodel, see page 51.)

A new face in front...
a new lath roof for the back patio

The simplest of face-lifting additions tidied up the looks of this house. The photos on this page show how a lath-type screen — together wtih painting and improved planting — unified and elongated the street face. The photos on the opposite page show how a shade structure was used in the back not only to improve the looks of the house but to provide needed protection against a hot summer sun. Its design repeats the screen effect produced in front.

A lath-type structure like this can be relatively lightweight. Since air passes freely through it, there is no engineering problem of holding it down in a high wind. Note how the beams are attached to the house rafters at one end, and at the other end to posts set beyond the concrete pad in a planting bed.

Design: T. W. McAllister & Associates.

Existing house: *a hodge-podge of lines and wall planes.*

Front of house *was smoothed out by addition of screen across windows. Screen serves as backdrop for pine in the container on platform. Painting and improved planting also helped to unify and elongate the street face.*

Overhead lath structure for back patio creates patterned shade and helps obscure a power pole (shown below, left), is attached to house rafters at one end, at other end to posts set in planting bed.

Existing patio was uninviting and uninteresting, with little planting and no protection from sun or wind.

Double beams (1 by 6-inch) of shade structure are bolted to either side of 4 by 4 posts with 2 by 2's on top.

The streetside was completely re-done

This house faces a heavily traveled street which curves around the property. And because the house faces southeast, the front lawn was the sunniest part of the garden—an ideal location for outdoor living, except for its complete lack of privacy.

The solution to this problem was to set up three tall baffles to screen the house from the street. Behind the baffles, a paved patio 36 feet wide and 20 feet deep easily accommodates lawn chairs and a picnic table.

Design: Glen Hunt.

Before remodel, *house on busy street lacked privacy.*

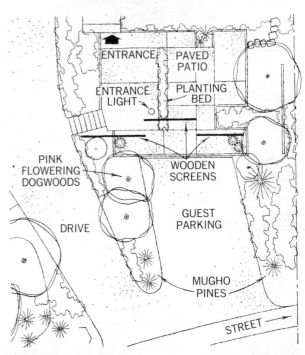

Plan shows *how new patio merges with new driveway.*

After remodel, *three tall baffles, each 12 feet wide, screen house from parking area and street. Behind them, new paved patio is 36 feet wide and 20 feet deep, has ample space for outdoor living.*

New roof, new windows... new inside stairwell

The remarkable thing about this remodeled house is how much it was changed in appearance, yet how little was done to alter its actual size and shape. (See *before* and *after* views on page 47.)

Refinished with natural cedar shingles with a new emphasis on its horizontal lines, and tied into the garden with terraced walls and steps, the house now fits even more comfortably into its wooded setting. Inside, the owners gained an interior stairwell and a protected entrance at ground level, and windows on all three levels that open up the walls to the south and west for all available sun and light. The new inside stairway also makes the ground floor level more accessible to the family room and to storage and furnace rooms.

Architect: Michael J. Soldano.

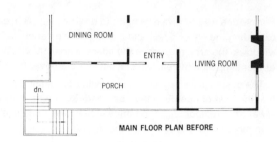

MAIN FLOOR PLAN BEFORE

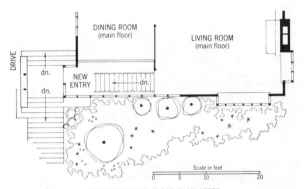

ENTRY AND MAIN FLOOR PLAN AFTER

New stairway *occupies space of former screened-in porch. Large windows at left replaced screens, provide same view.*

New entry *is on the lower level. A baffle opposite the door directs people to the steps leading down at both sides.*

A new face...a cooler house

Here is one way to give new spirit to a fairly plain, 30-year-old house. By extending the eaves 5 feet and placing lattice panels in front of the windows, the architects gave the house a smooth, veranda-like face, further simplified by removal of a bulky roofed-over front porch.

The design is well suited to areas with hot summers. The owners found that the cost of operating their air conditioner was considerably lower after remodeling. The lattice panels also eliminate sky glare and give more privacy to rooms on the street.

Architects: Moring and Billing.

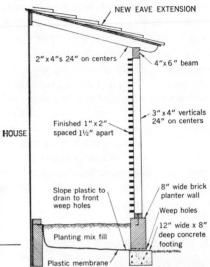

NEW EAVE EXTENSION

2" x 4"s 24" on centers

4" x 6" beam

HOUSE

Finished 1" x 2" spaced 1½" apart

3" x 4" verticals 24" on centers

Slope plastic to drain to front weep holes

8" wide brick planter wall

Weep holes

Planting mix fill

12" wide x 8" deep concrete footing

Plastic membrane

Sketch *of original house shows lack of roof overhang. Outside walls were fully exposed to summer sun — a major concern in areas with hot summers.*

Plastic membrane *under the planting mix fill drains water away from the foundation.*

House was painted *a light avocado color to blend in with cork oaks and birches. Extended eaves and lattice panels in front of windows help to eliminate sky glare and provide additional privacy from street.*

Used-brick entry replaced narrow concrete walk. Planting beds are filled with crushed white rock to emphasize the shape of shrubs and other plants. Low wall of used brick to right of entry forms planter bed.

Raised bed is protected by wide overhang and lattice panels; planting shows up dramatically between panels.

Behind panels large lights are suspended from overhang to illuminate plantings against the green house.

A unified roof line and a new living room window

The new roof dominates in making this a handsome house, but its looks are not its only justification. The hip-and-gable form unifies a formerly jumbled roofline and adds 4-foot protective overhangs on all sides— kept from dropping too low over windows by a flattened pitch at the eave line.

The latticelike gable opening above ventilates the attic space. The living room window was enlarged but to avoid an excessive amount of glare without reducing the light quality, shoji panels were placed over the glass on each side.

Architect: Vladimir Ossipoff.

Original exterior had random roof and window lines.

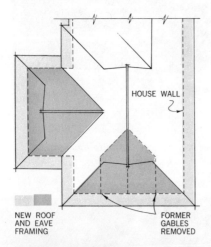

HOUSE WALL

NEW ROOF AND EAVE FRAMING

FORMER GABLES REMOVED

Window openings on each side of large living room window use fiberglass shoji.

New hip-and-gable roof soars gracefully over the house, extending sheltering overhangs on all sides. New exterior siding is maintenance-free asbestos-cement board applied directly over the old siding.

A new entry garden for bedroom privacy

What altered the character of this small house was nothing more than a fence that squared off an L formed by the house and garage — but it made a big difference.

The new fence gained for the owners a private garden area which helped to isolate the front bedroom, making a pleasant, enclosed retreat between it and traffic noise. The new landscaping and the new façade helped to make the height of the house seem more in proportion to its width and better related to its site.

Architects: Matlin and Dvoretzky.

Before. House had jumble of lines and windows.

— EXISTING WALLS
---- NEW WALLS

0 5 10

After. Façade is unified, enlarged by fence and painting, has clean lines.

Garden beside entry creates a private, bowerlike outlook for the bedrooms.

New facade is created by fencing two sides of L formed by house and garage. Overhead structure relates garden to the house by obscuring the high eave line.

A new screen wall to give improved privacy

Wanting to make more out of their front yard, the owners found they could improve the looks of their house and surrounding property and at the same time gain usable outdoor space.

They added a private patio off the existing front bedroom. To do this, they replaced a window with a sliding glass door. For privacy they erected a pierced concrete block wall (8 by 8 by 8-inch blocks with open cores), which lets in light and does not completely cut off their view of the street.

A solid wall between the patio and the entry perpendicular to the concrete block wall provides privacy. This wall and a new lattice overhead — which shades both patio and entry — combine to form a courtyard garden that dramatizes the entry.

The house had seemed somewhat uncomfortable on its site because of the high front bank. The new landscaping added terraces retained by low concrete block walls, reducing the bank to flat planes and gentler slopes. The planting also emphasizes the horizontal line.

Architects: Matlin and Dvoretzky.

Existing house had no continuous horizontal line to tie it together; front yard was unbroken slope away from the entry.

New lines and planes work together to emphasize horizontal, making house seem firmly planted on site. Patio wall, trellis extend lines of garage; slope is terraced into nearly horizontal planes, has new planting.

OPENING THE HOUSE
TO OUTDOOR LIVING

Former back wing of this house had difficult access to outdoors, did not take advantage of garden outlook. New L-shaped deck is used to connect new glass wall of living room and remodeled wing. It provides outdoor passageway and outdoor living under the branches of spreading oaks. Glass wall opens up new family room, makes it easy to move in and out. (For coverage of this remodel, see page 61.)

New deck creates a garden room

The owners of this house liked its location and the interior arrangement was workable. Their problem was how to create more suitable outdoor living space.

They found that between the detached front garage and the living room there was space for a garden court. The house's deep setback from the street also suggested a private garden off the master bedroom in front. On the south side, the rear garden could hold a pool.

Building decks at floor level makes it easy to move in and out to a new garden room and to the rear garden. Fencing across the front created a private bedroom garden and unified the façade. New sliding glass doors opened up the master bedroom and living, dining, and breakfast rooms to the outdoors.

Architect: Alfred T. Wilkes.

Before. *The garage was detached and situated in front of the L-shaped house. The existing courtyard was not exploited. Note the small window openings.*

After. *Trellis and fencing tie the garage into a unified façade. Master bedroom looks out on private garden.*

Garden room *is created by broad new deck, trellis, entry gate, fence, and the re-clad wall of the garage.*

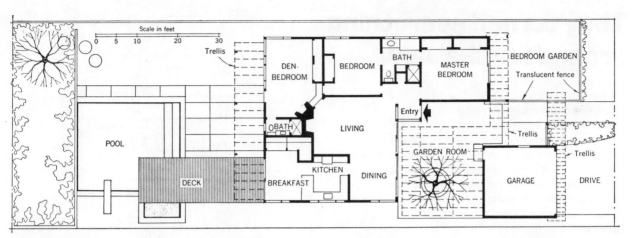

Floor and plot plan *shows new deck areas near bedroom, dining room, and the pool; easy access to the outdoors.*

Sliding glass doors *lead to large deck, pool, and back yard. Floor plane of kitchen and breakfast room continues out to deck and garden beyond to enlarge the living area of the house and add to the feeling of spaciousness.*

They turned everything around for the view

The outdoor living area of this house faced into a hill, on the side of the house away from the view. The owners wanted a better orientation. To achieve this, the architect designed some changes inside and out. The entry was changed from front (the view side) to back. A generous deck was substituted for the original entry porch; a narrow extension of the deck outside the kitchen and master bedroom makes it accessible from those rooms as well. Inside, the old entry hall and coat closet were incorporated into the dining room, and the lanai became a spacious entry hall.

Architect: Edwin Wadsworth.

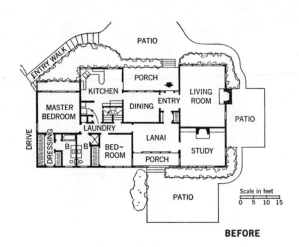

BEFORE

Original back patio was planned as an outdoor living area with house as protection against wind, was viewless.

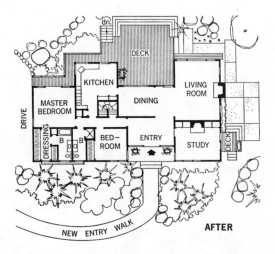

AFTER

New entry walk is behind small pines at the left. Patio at right is reached through new sliding glass door. New deck is on opposite side of house (hidden by planting), provides outdoor living with panoramic view.

New glass walls and deck
bring the garden indoors

After living several years in an old house which they had bought because they fell in love with the trees, the owners decided to remodel. (See page 57 for views of the house *before* and *after* remodeling.) Their primary objective was to open the house more to the outdoors. They accomplished this by adding a glass wall to the living room to blend in with new glass walls of a new family room (former unused bedroom). A floor-level deck connects these two rooms and provides an outdoor passageway and outdoor living under a spreading oak.

Architect: H. Douglas Byles.

SCALE IN FEET
0   5   10

DECK

FAMILY ROOM

BEDROOM

GALLERY

BEDROOM

KITCHEN

ORIGINAL BATH

ORIGINAL
PANTRY

ORIGINAL SERVICE PORCH

OLD WALLS

Original gallery *served as a hallway and dining room.*

Floor plan *shows the former walls, rooms in gray tone.*

New family room *and dining area is pleasantly open to garden. It serves for parties or for more intimate family use. Pegged hardwood floor is uncarpeted and used for dancing. Acoustical ceiling controls sound.*

Expanded living area...spacious outdoor feeling

This remodeling project achieved three major results — it squeezed a swimming pool into a very limited space, expanded the living area out to the lot lines, and opened the house to a garden redesigned to be seen and used more.

To integrate indoor and outdoor areas and bring a spacious feeling into a crowded situation, the architect opened up the house and its extensions along a diagonal line from the living room to the outer left corner of the lot. He made the pool an integral part of a brick terrace to unify the outdoor space. To bring the garden nearer and to create a buffer in the 3-foot space between house and pool, the remodel plan substituted plant material for a third of the former lanai. The new lanai roof is partly a trellis carried around the corner of the dining room, which has a new glass end wall. Living and dining rooms and master bedroom now open wide to the terrace.

Architect: Thomas O. Wells.

Brick paving comes right up to edge of the pool, also extends into lanai without interruption, enhancing the effect of spaciousness. New lanai roof is partly a trellis carried around corner of dining room.

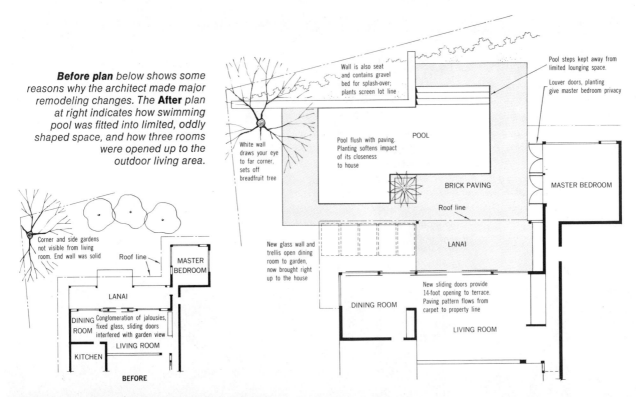

Before plan *below shows some reasons why the architect made major remodeling changes. The* **After** *plan at right indicates how swimming pool was fitted into limited, oddly shaped space, and how three rooms were opened up to the outdoor living area.*

Corner and side gardens not visible from living room. End wall was solid

Roof line

MASTER BEDROOM

LANAI

DINING ROOM — Conglomeration of jalousies, fixed glass, sliding doors interfered with garden view

KITCHEN

LIVING ROOM

BEFORE

Wall is also seat and contains gravel bed for splash-over; plants screen lot line

Pool steps kept away from limited lounging space.

Louver doors, planting give master bedroom privacy

White wall draws your eye to far corner, sets off breadfruit tree

Pool flush with paving. Planting softens impact of its closeness to house

POOL

BRICK PAVING

MASTER BEDROOM

Roof line

New glass wall and trellis open dining room to garden, now brought right up to the house

LANAI

New sliding doors provide 14-foot opening to terrace. Paving pattern flows from carpet to property line

DINING ROOM

LIVING ROOM

Living room view *is through lanai to pool area. The garden is framed by a 9½-foot-wide overhead which is part solid, part open. Low, white wall beyond defines pool, draws eye across pool to garden.*

This house now opens to the pool

Although this looks like an extensive remodel, total floor space in
this house was increased only by a 3½-foot extension on the master bedroom,
and a new family room. But observe how skillfully the house has been
opened up to the swimming pool and to new shaded and sunny terrace areas.

To meet the need for more floor space, the architect designed a
family room at the same level as the existing living room, 18 inches lower
than the floor in the rest of the house. His design removed the wall
between the living and dining rooms and opened the new
family room to the library (former music room).

Two bedrooms and the study now open to the pool area with sliding glass
doors in place of former windows. The addition of a floor-level deck
facilitates passage outside and makes the rooms look larger.

Architect: Carl Day.

Overlooking pool, rear-facing bedrooms have sliding glass doors. The floor level of each room exits to an engawa-
like veranda that shelters glass against the rays of the sun and bright reflection from the pool.

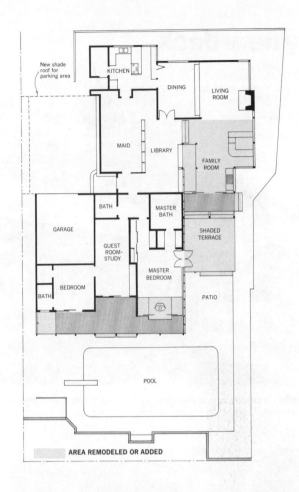

Former patio area became new family room, with barbecue and entertainment facilities, brick floor.

Family room opens to new shaded terrace, sunny patio beyond. Note lattice facing on house wall (right).

Master bedroom addition is big enough for fireplace, sitting space, and veranda; has dropped ceiling.

Outdoor living expanded by new deck

This house fronts a lake where the owners like to entertain and enjoy outdoor living. With four growing children they wanted to expand their house to the out-of-doors.

Two stories high on the downhill side, the main living rooms and entry to the house were situated on the upper level with narrow windows breaking up the view. On the lower level was a small, unfinished playroom; a conventional door led to narrow terraces and paths. With such limited access it was not easy to reach the water, or even to use the outdoor area.

The architect designed a large deck and broad steps from the upper terrace down to the seawall level. He also opened the lower floor into a large patio room, complete with a small kitchen, so the new space could be used all year. Upstairs, wider windows and a new rail opened the living room to a view of the lake.

The deck gave the owners something new: a large level area for outdoor living. The broad steps make it easy to reach the water and also provide generous extra seating for guests.

Architect: Burr Richards.

Before remodeling, *two-story house had large glass areas facing the lake, but no easy access to the water.*

After remodeling, *house had widened view and access openings on upper level. On lower level, new patio room opens to new outdoor sun deck. Broad steps lead down from deck to water, provide extra seating.*

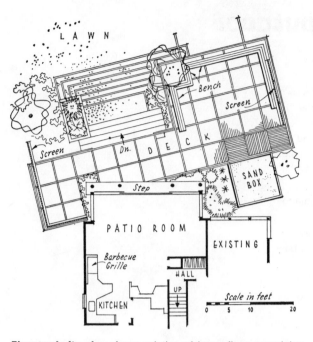

Floor and site plan shows relation of lower floor remodel to new deck and steps and to lakeside lawn area.

Playroom wall opens to deck—glass rolls away to leave 12-foot-wide opening. Wide steps extend floor level.

Sun deck replaces former narrow terrace across the face of house. Fir log posts repeat dock piling, deck support posts.

Eating counter separates a new playroom from the kitchen. Dropped kitchen ceiling has built-in down lights.

This deck makes indoor-outdoor space a step apart

With a fine view of the lake from the rear of their hillside house, the owners had no convenient way to enjoy it outdoors. The architect overcame this lack by adding a new deck outside a new dining room.

Originally, there was a concrete patio in the location the deck and dining room now occupy. To reach this patio, the owners had to make a roundabout trip through the back door and the carport, around the north side of the house.

Sliding glass doors were installed to give direct access from the house to a new and generous outdoor living space. At the same time the dining room was opened to the view and to the light.

The deck is really three decks in one. The largest area has built-in benches and space enough to accommodate a large group. Joining this space is a somewhat more secluded area, for an outdoor table and chairs. The third section is more of a balcony that continues the deck line across the west face of the house.

Architect: Burr Richards.

Deck is shaded at one end by new dining room's north wall while benches of other section are in the sun. Decking is redwood 2 by 4's in 4-foot squares, adds 480 square feet of level area with view of lake.

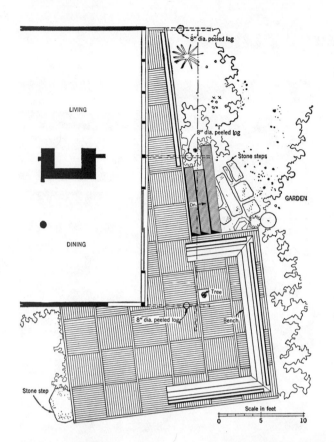

Corridor extension of deck has access to dining room sliding glass doors; living room entrance is beyond.

Steps lead up to deck and new dining room doors beyond. On this section of deck, the bench acts as a protective rail. Use of peeled log poles contributes a rustic effect, augmented by natural finish of deck.

A comfortable place to enjoy the view

Remodeling which results in the better use of outdoor areas can be just as important to the livability and appearance of your home as improvements made in the house itself. The addition of this spacious deck makes the adjoining family room appear much larger, as well as giving the family a comfortable place outdoors to enjoy the view. The space beneath the deck serves as a carport. Corrugated aluminum suspended under deck joists directs rain runoff, keeps the car dry.

Design: Glen Hunt.

Before addition the house had no outdoor living area.

Deck is screened from the street, open to view at right.

New deck forms roof for a carport, adds large, convenient outdoor living room, and improves the looks of the house.

REMODELING THE GRACIOUS OLD-TIMERS

Style of original house was Dutch Colonial —
one that the owners wished to retain but
improve with a fresh new roof, siding, and
entryway (the only structural addition). Narrow
windows of new entryway blend with
ones of original living room (see photo below).
New fencing separates parking area (right)
from houses next door, also screens
entryway. (For details on the handsome interior
finishing of this house, see page 80.)

From a two-story box to a more livable home

This remodeled house is so delightful, it's hard to imagine it as it was — a stiff, two-story box shape with an English Tudor façade, typical of the 1920's. The owners lived in it for 13 years before its inconvenient room arrangement became unbearable. But they liked their urban location for its convenience and quiet, so they decided to remodel.

Originally the front garden was a large lawn bisected by a concrete path to the front door. It became a brick-paved and enclosed garden, entered from the driveway. The tiny entrance hall was widened and lengthened to handle the main traffic on the first floor. The living and dining rooms were joined and opened to the solarium, the real hub of the house. Upstairs, the master bedroom was equipped with a new dormer and skylight and a small balcony.

Architects: A. O. Bumgardner & Partners.

Entrance *to remodeled 1920 house is via walkway and iron gate beyond.*

New bedroom dormer *with balcony overlooks brick-paved garden and patio. Trellis shades low deck in front of the house.*

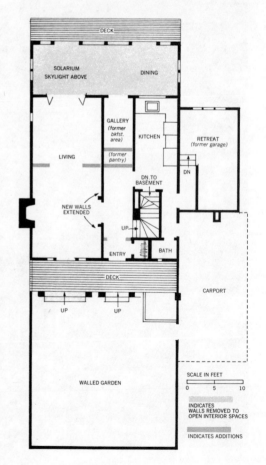

DECK

SOLARIUM
SKYLIGHT ABOVE

DINING

GALLERY
(former
bkfst.
area)

KITCHEN

RETREAT
(former garage)

LIVING

(former
pantry)

DN. TO
BASEMENT

DN

NEW WALLS
EXTENDED

UP.

ENTRY

BATH

DECK

CARPORT

UP

UP

WALLED GARDEN

SCALE IN FEET
0   5   10

INDICATES
WALLS REMOVED TO
OPEN INTERIOR SPACES

INDICATES ADDITIONS

Master bedroom *has new soaring ceiling and skylight.*

Solarium-dining area *is at rear of house; has skylight.*

New entrance hall *handles traffic on first floor; is also used as a picture gallery. Floor is of polished brick pavers and runs from the front door to the solarium. Living room is through door at left, stairway at right.*

The plan called for step-by-step remodeling

In this remodel there was no attempt to retain any of the character of the existing house, a stucco bungalow built in the 1920's. In fact, every effort was made to alter its appearance and to make it blend more naturally with its woodland setting. Another goal was to create a better indoor-outdoor relationship; the small high-sill windows had only limited views into the woods and kept out the light and warmth of the low winter sun.

The master plan for the remodeling divided it into four phases. The first phase called for landscaping and repaving of the back garden and terrace. The second updated the kitchen with new equipment, countertops, and sink. The third phase required the greatest amount of alteration. It involved adding an entry hall, extending the living room on two sides (see plan), and replacing the bedroom bay. The extensions gained only 170 square feet of space, but it was highly usable space. The final phase added two bedrooms and converted an existing bedroom to a second bath.

Architect: Barry G. Smith.

Before. *House was oriented to street, had no outdoor area.*

After. *House was given not just a face-lifting, but a total change in appearance to suit setting. The long, narrow windows make the interior considerably lighter, provide view of the tall trees beyond.*

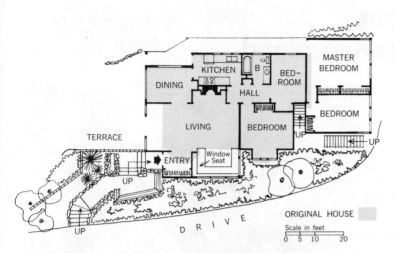

Unshaded area shows changes and additions to house containing entry hall, window seat in living room, and two new bedrooms.

Wall of living room was extended to create space for window seat. New windows provide good view of redwoods and creek.

Terrace off living room has high fence for complete privacy from street. Overhang of roof helps to shade glass doors.

Entry hall has brick pavers extended from the outside entrance, natural stone wall at the right.

Updated inside and out but Spanish character retained

Roomy and well built, this Mediterranean-style house needed remodeling to suit it to family living today. Though updated inside and out, it still retains much of its characteristic Spanish-American flavor.

Working closely with the owners, the architects offset the rather boxlike look of the house by designing a generous tile-covered entry and a wide carport to replace the rather insignificant detached garage. They added a family room (see plan) which in effect switched the house orientation from front to back, to take advantage of a new outdoor living area created in place of the old garage.

Windows in most of the rooms were enlarged to let in ample light, with considerable use of louvered glass for better ventilation.

Architects: Benton & Park.

Old house had charm but wasn't planned for family living today.

Remodeled house has carport extension to elongate the line; the raised bed in front makes the house look lower.

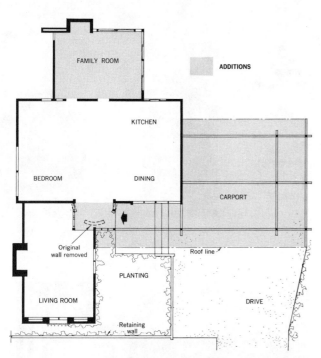

Interior changes *included redesigning the entry, enlarging kitchen, and adding family room at the back.*

Family room opens *onto spacious patio on site once occupied by the garage; patio has trellis overhead.*

Former entry *was small and dark with narrow steps.*

New entry *is protected by overhang; has broad steps.*

A 56-year-old house begins its second life

The character that only age can give a house and its setting is sometimes more important than how well the house works. The owners of this 56-year-old house bought it for just such character, with the idea of remodeling. Their problem was two-fold: First, each room downstairs was a kind of hallway, and second, subdivision of the area had left the house with no street side entry. The addition of an entry solved both these problems (see plans).

The remodeling also included giving the kitchen an arched window over the breakfast table to gain openness and light.

The end wall of the living room was closed off from the playroom, the stairway was removed, and the entrance was moved — all helping to reduce traffic and make furniture arrangement much easier.

Architect: Henrik Bull.

Entry hall *has front door at the far left; door beyond leads to storage area.*

Remodeled kitchen *has view of deck from sink and breakfast counter, is screened from the hallway by swinging door.*

Former kitchen *seemed quite confining. Although it had three doors, none of them led to the outside.*

Living room *is given new character by wood paneling on the walls; door from hall is to the left of fireplace.*

Former living room *was long in proportion to the width; many doors made furniture arrangement difficult.*

South side of house shows living room bay window. To its right was original entry; in remodeling, arched doors with plate glass panels replaced French doors, porch roof was added. Playroom entry is at left.

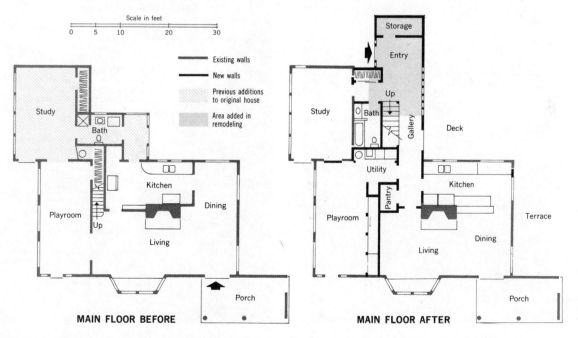

Scale in feet

0   5   10   20   30

Existing walls
New walls
Previous additions to original house
Area added in remodeling

Study

Bath

Playroom

Up

Kitchen

Dining

Living

Porch

MAIN FLOOR BEFORE

Storage

Entry

Up

Study

Bath

Gallery

Deck

Utility

Playroom

Pantry

Kitchen

Terrace

Living

Dining

Porch

MAIN FLOOR AFTER

Floor plans of main floor. Note that before remodeling each room had three doors to other rooms and closets, were open to continued traffic. House had no workable entry, and stairway entered living room.

New life for an old Dutch Colonial

The transformation of this small (865 square feet) Dutch Colonial-style house was by the architect-owner and his wife. Except for help in roughing-in the entry way (the only structural addition), the owners did all the work themselves (see page 71 for *before* and *after* views.) The photographs shown below suggest the extent and quality of finished detailing throughout the house.

Architect: Harrell McCarty.

Entry hall is spacious and airy, provides coat storage. Stairs in the foreground lead up to living-dining room.

Cabinet finishing matches that of deck counter in kitchen. Unglazed ceramic tile covers the old floors.

Walls, cabinets in bathroom, elsewhere in house are random cedar mill ends (1 to 3 feet long) with cedar plugs.

The owners liked the location, but...

The little house shown at right was built in 1940. The owners always liked its location, but found that they needed more room.

First they added a second story to gain separate bedrooms for their growing children. Then, by pushing one living room wall out toward the street, they were able to add a new and bigger living room and provide greater separation between the living and dining rooms. The former living room became a music room.

The architect also designed a new entry screen and suggested opening up the wall between the dining room and hall with glass. A built-in buffet provides dining room storage; cornice lights illuminate both sides of the screen.

Architect: Henrik Bull.

Original *house was small, had one story.*

New living room *ceiling is changed from a flat, low ceiling of original house. Bay window exploits view beyond.*

Remodeled dining area *has a new screen of redwood and patterned glass; its light illuminates the stair well.*

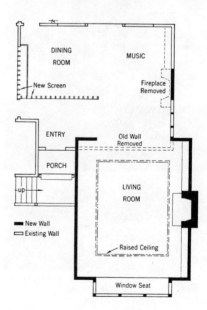

New wing *at right projects out toward the street with bay window on living room level. Trellislike roof extension was repeated on original building.*

Suitable to their needs, but it needed updating

It was more than sentiment that led the owners of this old family house to remodel. They took a long look at new houses for sale and found none had the right space arrangement. The old house did: It had a separate dining room, a bedroom and bath on the main living level, and two additional bedrooms and a bath on the second level, which could be closed off when not needed for guests.

A certain amount of remodeling and face lifting, however, was needed. The photograph below shows how the front of the house was altered and landscaped. Inside, the major changes involved a complete gutting and remodeling of the kitchen and the addition of a bay window. With the exception of some new storage closets, the other interior spaces were refurbished, not altered.

Design: W. K. Huntington.

Before. *Space inside was just right but the house was dark.*

New bay window *brings additional light into living room; new entry is at left. Front porch was removed to make room for generous-sized deck for outdoor sitting and entertaining. House was given new coat of paint.*

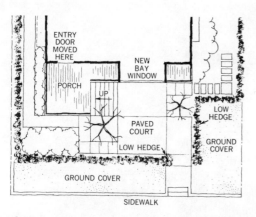

Ground cover and the paved court replaced the front lawn.

Bay window replaced three small windows, is large enough to hold a full-length sofa and two end tables.

New kitchen has oak cabinets and a tile floor. Counters are surfaced with ceramic tile, wood, and marble.

Entry steps were turned sideways, are partly screened from the streetside traffic by a large star magnolia.

Extensive remodeling without altering the basic shape

Built in the 1890's, this house looked like the sketch at right before it was remodeled. It is a very good example of what can be done by extensive remodeling without altering the existing house shape. To the architect, the redesign of this house for his own use was a welcome challenge that required a good deal of architectural discipline.

The existing house was a modified Dutch colonial. To dramatize the characteristic roof shape, he removed a dormer and the porch which had been added sometime after the house was built. He added a smaller dormer to provide cross-ventilation upstairs, but it does not disrupt the roofline. In effect the dormer and new chimney are designed to play up the gambrel roof.

One reason for buying the house was the view, best from bedroom windows at the back of the house (see plan). The upper floor was reorganized to take advantage of this view, and the two back bedrooms became the living room, opened to the view.

Architect: A. O. Bumgardner.

Sketch of original house built in the 1890's. Roof line was jumbled, garage too small for today's larger cars.

After remodeling house had a new roof dormer to provide cross-ventilation upstairs, new private garden.

Deck outside entry adjoins the dining area and kitchen; continues around side of house at right.

BEFORE
UPPER LEVEL

AFTER
UPPER LEVEL   650 sq. ft.

Comparing Before *and* **After** *plans, note how the interior spaces were reorganized but baths and kitchen didn't change positions. Space occupied on the upper level by bedrooms was used for new living room with large window facing the view.*

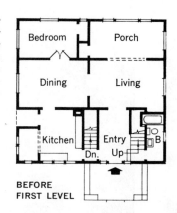

BEFORE
FIRST LEVEL

Scale in feet
0   10   20

AFTER
FIRST LEVEL   1195 sq. ft.

Bedroom *on upper level opens into living area, gets natural light from new dormer (left background).*

Living area *is separated from bedroom by wardrobe-room divider. Fixtures atop divider give indirect light.*

REMODELING OLD-TIMERS   85

This old Victorian
was opened up for outdoor living

This old Victorian house had no notable moldings, fireplaces, paneling, or finishes worth retaining. But the intrinsic quality of the basic architecture — high ceilings, tall, double hung windows, the original façade — was retained and exploited. Within the original shell the remodeling achieved a contemporary feeling reminiscent of the Victorian tradition but not adhering strictly to it.

During World War II, the house had been converted to three apartments, but after the architect re-established the upper floor as a single family unit, the space occupied by the back apartment was turned into an outdoor living area.

Architect: Herbert D. Kosovitz.

Front of house got new paint. Only structural addition was a 6-foot-high wall around garage roof to screen sitting area.

Trellis system in the background is over area that was once part of rear apartment. Solid wall at right screens the area.

Dining area opens to deck through glass door at the left, balanced by fixed window on the opposite side.

Skylit part of sitting area is 15 feet high. The central hall, beyond, is flanked by bookshelves, storage units.

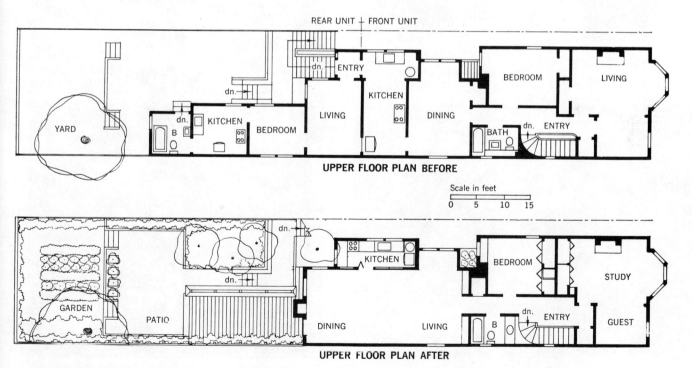

REAR UNIT ┼ FRONT UNIT

UPPER FLOOR PLAN BEFORE

Scale in feet
0   5   10   15

UPPER FLOOR PLAN AFTER

New kitchen was swung off to one side, utilizing space once used for entry to a rear apartment. Two interior walls were removed to create one large dining-living area. Former living room at front is now study.

A new family room and sheltered patio

Remodeling of this old house involved rearranging and updating an obsolete kitchen and adding a family room. The family room provides easy access to a sheltered brick patio outside.

The small lavatory off the back entry (see *before* plan) was removed; in its place is one entrance to the family room and a pass-through from the kitchen to the hall.

The remodeled kitchen opens to the family room, but a feeling of partial separation is achieved by a counter peninsula with cook top and storage on both sides.

Architect: Adolph S. Rosekrans.

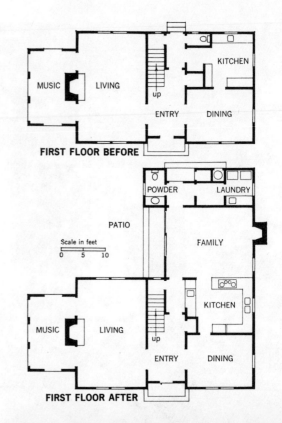

FIRST FLOOR BEFORE

FIRST FLOOR AFTER

Cooking counter separates the family room from the kitchen, has wood top. Sink top at the right is plastic laminate.

New addition, at left, opens directly to brick patio through sliding glass door; open window is in new bath.

Exposed beams of living room give solid look; the large skylight above provides additional light. Floors are of quarry tile.

MAKING A HOUSE OUT OF A NON-HOME

Old store had been boarded up for years. A close inspection revealed sturdy framework that would support remodel. As the photo below shows, the original lines of store remain (minus false front that obscured gable). Basement, excavated under existing structure, was fitted out as sleeping quarters. (To see how the building was converted, see page 93.)

Comfortable outdoor room was once a garage

The uncommonly interesting house shown here once was an uncommon three-car garage on a wooded hill section of an old estate. But its interest lies less in its origins than in the environment it creates and the exciting quality it achieves by exploiting vertical space. Out from the shell of the original building a bold two-story screen structure gives a soaring, airy feeling. It allows the main part of the house to be in touch with fresh air, sky, and trees that direct the eye upward. The outdoor room this structure creates is another living room, dining room, party room, entry, and hallway. Planned as part of this indoor-outdoor complex is the swimming pool below, dominating the garden view and contributing to an atmosphere of carefree living.

Indoors, the house has a large, informal living-dining area and bedrooms that have the feeling of separate apartments, in contrast with the large group-living spaces. Foot traffic between parts of the house can move either indoors or outdoors.

Design: John I. Matthias.

Former garage had complete apartment on the upper level.

Remodeled structure has a dramatic, two-story screened front that encloses a main-level outdoor living-dining room and an upper deck. Paved area beside pool expands available entertaining area for large parties.

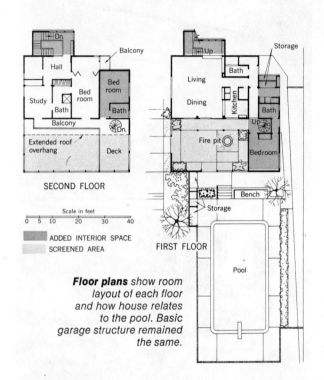

Floor plans *show room layout of each floor and how house relates to the pool. Basic garage structure remained the same.*

SECOND FLOOR

Dn.
Hall
Study
Bath
Bed room
Bedroom
Bath
Balcony
Balcony
Extended roof overhang
Deck

Scale in feet
0 5 10 20 30 40

ADDED INTERIOR SPACE
SCREENED AREA

FIRST FLOOR

Up
Bath
Storage
Living
Dining
Kitchen
Bath
Up
Dn.
Fire pit
Bedroom
Bench
Storage
Pool

Two-story stairwell *continues the bookshelf walls.*

Living room *gives a pleasant sense of enclosure in contrast to the open, vertical spaces to which it opens on both sides. Two-story stairwell is three steps up at right rear, has room for large game table.*

(Continued on next page)

**...Comfortable outdoor room
was once a garage (continued)**

Party area of garden room has firepit. Pass-through from the kitchen is convenient for easy serving.

Outdoor dining area has large table that can be expanded to accommodate a large number of guests.

Kitchen has a second pass-through to indoor dining room. This opening can be closed off with folding shutters.

Old country store is now a shore-side cabin

More than 50 years old, this was a country store in dilapidated condition but sound enough to become a pleasant summer cottage. When the owners first saw the building, it was covered with moss and leaves and surrounded by rank growth. But close inspection revealed that the roof did not leak and the structure was sturdy and dry. (Photos on page 89 show how the structure looked *before* and *after* remodeling.)

The remodeling started with removing the square corners of the false front and a rotting lean-to. Then a basement was dug and walled with concrete block to make dormitory space with an outside stairway to reach it. The large single room on the main floor was subdivided into kitchen, bath, living-dining, and dressing rooms. Windows were added on the side facing the view. The building's first plumbing and new wiring, roofing, and flooring finished the job.

New deck overlooks bay, is level with floor of house for easy movement in and out. Trees at left shade it from afternoon sun and glare off water. Plastic overhead (not shown) shelters about a third of it.

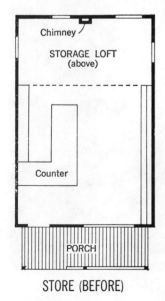

STORE (BEFORE)

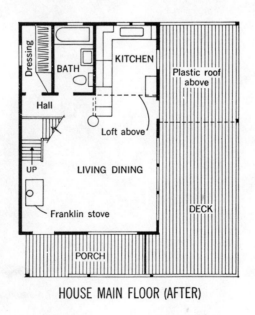

HOUSE MAIN FLOOR (AFTER)

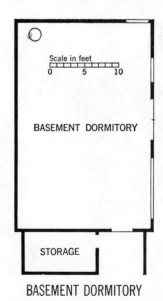

BASEMENT DORMITORY

A house that once was a four-car garage

This house was once a four-car garage for an old estate. Now it has been remodeled to become a handsome, highly livable residence. In a sense it epitomized the remodeling problem, for it was just about a pure instance of the rectangular box. Since the garage was built in the same stone style as the estate house, the handsome façade could be left mostly intact. One garage door opening became the entry, with a double front door and openwork brick on either side.

The structure used to contain garage and shop space below and living quarters above. Half of the garage space became an entry hall, living room, and dining area. Stairs were added inside for access to the second-story bedrooms and den. The old shop behind the remaining garage became the kitchen and utility room with a small bath.

Architects: Edwards-Pitman.

Façade *was little changed except for the new entry (former garage door opening).*

Large rear garden *now has a shady terrace off the dining room. Balcony is part of old apartment above the garage.*

GARAGE

B | UP
UTILITY
KIT.

UP

ENTRY | LIVING | DINING | TERRACE

LOWER FLOOR

Scale in feet
0   5   10

BATH | BEDROOM
BATH
BEDROOM
DN. | DN.
DEN | SITTING ROOM | PORCH

UPPER FLOOR

Single pane window *under the stairwell enlarges the garden view from the sink.*

Bookshelves *under stairway are handy to living-sitting area.*

Entry *has double front doors set between ventilation doors.*

They live in a former country schoolhouse

If a building is structurally sound — has good timbers — and the lines are good, it may be well worth remodeling. This house, for example, was an old schoolhouse built about 1886. When the owners bought it, it was simply a one-room structure. To make it into a residence, they added a kitchen, entry hall, and bath. Above these they added a bedroom with large dormer windows.

The photographs below and those on the next page show how they opened up one side of the living room with glass and an exterior deck, and how they used interior shutters to provide privacy.

Design: Roy Rydell.

Before. *Schoolhouse had small windows and entry.*

After. *Side wall is opened up wide with fixed glass and double doors. New wood deck and steps face garden and woods beyond.*

Entry hall *has floor covering that seems to draw guests inside; stairway to the bedroom is at right.*

Spacious living room seems even larger with the added glass. Windows at either side are two of the original three. Raised platform at far right is where school teacher had her desk. Dining table was made of local redwood.

Open shutters fold flat against the window frame, and do not obstruct outside view or keep daylight out.

Closed shutters give privacy, reduce loss of heat through the glass. Upper and lower sections work independently.

A new life for an old schoolhouse

This little Hawaiian building is a classic example of Island plantation housing of the 1920's. It also served as a judo hall, hula dance studio, health center, and schoolhouse. The owners converted the building into a two-bedroom home and studio without altering its original lines. The plan below shows how they divided the interior space.

Old recessed porch took up valuable inside space.

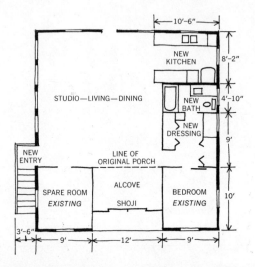

Remodeling moved entry to side, cut depth of porch.

Major living area contains dining, sleeping, and studio areas. Shoji screen opens to the front porch and the view.

IMPROVING THE SMALL SUBDIVISION HOUSE

Example of a subdivision remodel shows what can be done to improve the appearance of a fairly plain-looking house by increasing space and adding an inviting façade (see page 101 for other views). The following pages present a collection of other remodeling ideas from a 15-year-old tract development. Some houses have been thoroughly transformed, others have simply been changed in appearance. Some have achieved real individuality.

Adding space also created a new facade

A tidier façade was an indirect result of adding two rooms to this corner-lot house. The architect resolved the conflict of roof lines by extending the large gable and by adding a hip-roof section from the new entry to a bedroom added at far right (see large photo below).

The chief goal was more space. Moving the walls out toward the corner made space for a family room and a new entry. Hallway space came partly from the addition, partly from existing bedrooms.

Architect: Raymond **Kappe**.

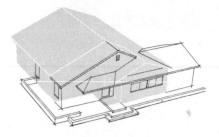

Former dining room *became family room, separated from the new entry hall by counter and folding partitions.*

Extra space *acquired by addition creates a new entry which leads to family room and new bedroom.*

Broad new entry steps *and walk are integrated with brick raised planting bed, make the facade seem lower and broader. House wall and entry door beyond were moved 8 feet toward camera (note floor-to-ceiling windows at left).*

Their old garage is now a music room

Here is a solution to the common problems of converting a garage to a family room (in this case a music room). A blank wall facing the street gives the new room privacy. High glass provides daylight, with balancing side light from a sliding glass door where the garage door used to be. A door in the new façade opens to a court that leads to the existing front entry. The new carport includes an open-work rear wall that helps light existing front windows while screening cars from their view.

All of these elements are unified in a design that reconciles the new flat roof with the existing gabled roof.

Design: R. Yarnelle McKay.

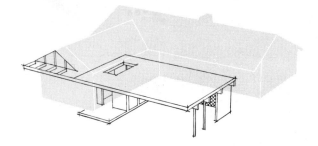

New music room has an acoustical plaster ceiling, carpeted floor, and ash paneled walls. Beyond this is the entry court.

Unbroken line of fascia unites elements of new room, enclosed entry court and the carport. In the carport, note the storage wall, open end with light steel posts, and screen block wall with existing windows at rear.

Garage was changed to a new family room

The owners of this house remodeled to make a family room out of their garage. They also remodeled the entry (for direct access to the new room and to take foot traffic out of the living room) and added a carport. They simply replaced the garage door with sliding glass doors and added finish floor, wall, and ceiling. Then they enclosed one part of their existing porch with patterned glass and extended the roof of the remainder of the porch horizontally for the car shelter.

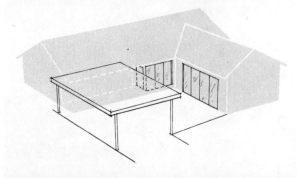

New entry has patterned glass for soft diffused light; isolates the living room from foot traffic to the kitchen.

New flat roof carport is anchored to the existing wall, supported on steel posts. Fascia is at same height as that of the existing porch. The former driveway is a new patio set off by container plants.

Added in front: two bedrooms and a hallway

The carefully worked out facade of this house resulted from a plan that makes maximum use of the former front yard in converting the garage to living space (see page 99 for *before* and *after* views).

By utilizing the old garage and adding onto it, they gained a large dormitory for three boys, a small guest bedroom, and bath. The addition's flat roof structure extends into an overhead for a new entry garden and a roof for a single carport.

Design: Doris Palmer Design Associates.

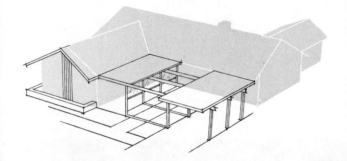

Entry garden *has lath shade. Gable at left marks the former garage which was expanded by half of its width.*

Entry, hall space *came from former bedroom (wall removed left, center) and porch (recess at front door). Hallway to kitchen and the new dormitory is behind chimney. Additional bedroom space was added at the rear of the house.*

More living space in front and in back

Despite the unusual lot, the way this house expanded in two directions is instructive to any prospective remodeler. One lesson: It is easier and less costly to add generous space to a gable-end wall than it is to expand from existing eaves, where the roof soon becomes too low or needs to be altered.

The remodeling also solved two common space deficiencies, providing a family room and also a bedroom and bath apartment for a relative. The former garage was an ideal spot for such an apartment — separate from the living area and from foot traffic, and reached by its own entrance.

The owners also added a new master bedroom at the rear of their old bedroom. Hall space to reach it came from the existing room, which they enlarged to make the new family room. They expanded the living-dining room into an existing rear porch, to accommodate foot traffic through it. A new concrete terrace provides an outdoor link for these three rooms.

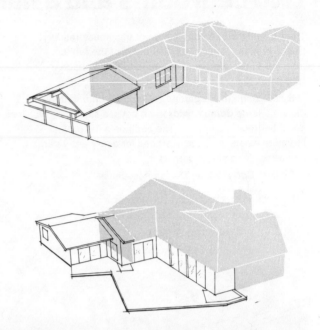

Carport added to gable of former garage at left is screened from street by pierced concrete block. At lower level, its roof lengthens and improves lines of house. Garage became apartment with separate entrance.

Concrete terrace links three rooms. New master bedroom (gable at left) was offset from existing gable-end wall to leave space for tall window in family room (center). Roof overhang of fiberglass plastic provides shelter for glass wall.

Living-dining room expanded to rear, creating more dining area, simplifying foot traffic. The family room door is at right. The new master bedroom at rear has sliding glass door opening to small extension of terrace.

A new family room was added in rear garden

The remodeling of the house shown on the previous two pages extended its rear L projection to make space for a family room. The remodeling of this house filled in the space at the rear to make a rectangle, with double gables that match the established roof slope. The existing structure provided two sides of a family room about 12 by 27 feet. This room takes informal activities and the clutter that attends living with small children out of the living room and puts them in direct view of the kitchen and within easy reach of the outdoors. The new room also provides light and a view for the living-dining room beyond.

Architects: Raymond L. Lloyd.

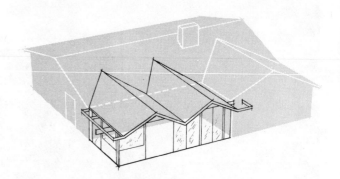

Double gables, glassed in, light new family room, make it seem loftier than it would with a flat ceiling, less barn-like than with a single large gable. Kitchen, around the corner to the right, now opens to rear view.

More living space...new master bedroom

There are several reasons for placing an addition in the rear. One is privacy (as example shows on opposite page). A second may be that the house expands naturally in that direction. A third may be simply that the house is on the setback line and cannot expand in front.

All three considerations influenced this remodeling. The owners added a new master suite (consisting of bedroom, bath, and dressing room) and a hall to reach it. They also extended their living room and their breakfast room to the rear. This added about 620 square feet of living space, two thirds of it in the master suite. Pleasant, airy, and in touch with a remodeled patio and garden, it more than compensates for the loss of usable outdoor space.

Architect: Raymond L. Lloyd.

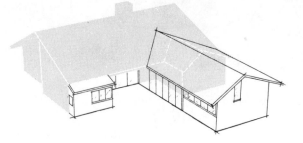

Master bedroom *turns away from the patio, opens with glass wall to a private side garden, a view shared by the new bath.*

Ceiling beam *in foreground marks line of former rear wall. Living room expanded to the line of former roofed porch, creating dining area off kitchen (door at right). Glassed-in hall reaches new master bedroom at rear.*

These two families spruced up on the streetside

The house shown at right presented the same face-lifting problem as the house shown below — it looked high, narrow, and boxy. The architects used simple means to lengthen and lower the lines of the façade, so the house seems more gracefully placed on its site. The horizontals and simplified forms contributed by the grillwork are reinforced by a long raised bed and a new entry walk.

Architects: Matlin & Dvoretzky.

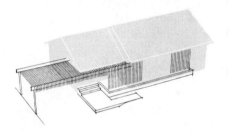

Grillwork screens half of porch, continues across front of arbor and porte cochère, establishes horizontal line and helps to simplify facade.

The house shown at right shows the simplest, least expensive way to tidy up a façade: Unify its lines with a simpler form. Here again the form is grillwork — a fence that matches the height of porch eave and window top. It encloses the porch on the front and side, shelters a small shade garden, and creates privacy for the windows behind without shutting out all the light or a view of the street. A new walk and a door in the fence clearly locate the entry.

(For more ideas on sprucing up the exterior of a house, see chapter entitled *Ideas for Exterior Face-lifting.)*

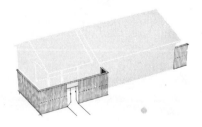

Entry fence simplifies, lengthens, and lowers apparent height of facade, is aided by the strong horizontal lines of low hedge and new planting.

PRACTICAL TIPS
FOR THE HANDYMAN

Installing a new ceiling

Two easy approaches are possible to remodeling a ceiling. Standard ceiling tile can be applied to an existing ceiling or joists, or panel-supporting grids can be hung below the joists to lower the ceiling. Suspended ceiling panels can be removed merely by lifting them from their grid supports, providing easy access to the actual ceiling for repairs to wiring or plumbing. Removal of tiles applied directly to the ceiling tends to be messy and difficult.

SUSPENDED PANEL CEILINGS

Suspended-grid paneled ceilings are by far the most adaptable for the do-it-yourselfer, since they can be installed a part at a time without repeated preparation or clean-up. One person can handle all operations, and mistakes are easily correctable. Components are replaceable.

Spring-type hangers which draw the grid up into contact with the joists and allow it to be pulled down for panel replacement have solved the problem of too-low ceilings. Portions of ceilings can be dropped for special uses without permanently affecting the rest of the ceiling. Transparent, translucent, or egg-crate grills can be used in place of normal acoustic or decorative tile to admit light from skylights or lighting fixtures above the panels.

Before You Start

Decide on the color, texture, and overall appearance you want in the panels and supporting grids. Choices include acoustic or decorative paneling, matching or contrasting supporting grids, minimal grid exposure, a recessed grid effect, or a heavy-beamed grid effect.

Next decide whether you want a dropped ceiling on wire or strap hangers or a ceiling flush with the joists on spring hangers.

If light-transmitting panels will be used, pick the lighting fixtures to be used with them. Some fixtures are designed for attachment to the original ceiling or joists, while others connect to grid supports.

To provide for through-the-ceiling ventilation fans or ducts, install the open kind of egg-crate grid panels that are used as light-transmitting panels.

Use flexible conduit between joist-mounted electrical junction boxes and moveable lighting and power outlet boxes or fixtures to permit greater flexibility in moving lighting and power fixtures. They can be moved anywhere in the grid within the reach of the flexible conduit.

Determine How Many Panels You Need

The easiest way to figure the number of panels you need is to use graph paper or a plain sheet of paper ruled into equal squares (any size). Measure wall lengths at the height at which the grid will hang and draw the ceiling area on the squared paper, using one square per foot of ceiling size. Block in the panel size you will be using and then count the blocked areas and parts of areas to get the number of panels you need.

For a professional looking job, the opposite borders of the room should be equal. To determine the non-standard width of panel needed for perimeter rows, take the number of inches left over in the long dimension after you have blocked in panel size. Add the length of a panel in inches and divide the sum by two. Repeat this procedure for the other room dimension.

Most ready-made panels are a fraction of an inch shorter in both length and breadth than the stated dimension, to allow for the space taken up by metal grid dividers. When using wooden grids with thick dividers, add ½ inch to stated panel dimensions for all layout and computation purposes. If you forget, most panel materials can be cut with a fine-toothed blade on a bench, radial, sabre, or hand saw.

Grid Installation—Not Difficult

Establish ceiling height by carefully drawing or snapping a chalk line on all four walls. Taking care to ensure level lines will prevent problems from out-of-line or wavy ceilings.

Main grid support rails should always run at right angles to the ceiling joists, which usually cross the short dimension of a room. Attach wall grid supports with top edges in line with the established ceiling height line. Lay out grid accurately by measuring and stretching strings from wall to wall—directions follow. This seemingly fussy approach can save panel fitting problems. Few walls are at true right angles to each other, and many are surprisingly wavy and out of plumb.

Pick a reference corner to work from; then measure the exact distance computed for perimeter panels at each end of the shorter wall. Insert a bent nail or hook at this point, and attach a string. Stretch the string to a hook inserted at a corresponding point in the opposite wall, with the string parallel to the long wall. Now measure from the reference corner along the long wall the distance computed for the other perimeter panel dimension, insert hook and string, and stretch string so that it is at right angles to the first string—not necessarily parallel to the short wall. Measure angle with a carpenter's square or use the 3-4-5 measurement method illustrated on page 112.

Hang first main support exactly in line with the longer string (at right angles to ceiling joists) and exactly level with the wall supports. Use the clips, hangers, or wires supplied by the manufacturer to hang the grid supports from the joists with no more than 4-foot intervals between hangers. It may be necessary to trim main grid supports so the first cross support connector matches the right angle made by

HOW TO INSTALL A SUSPENDED CEILING

Determine new ceiling height, then mark with a chalk line. Fasten molding to walls so bottom of molding is on the chalk line.

Install screw eyes in existing ceiling structure, attach steel hanger wires, and fasten the wires to the grid support rails.

Attach cross supports to the grid support runners, then rest ceiling panels on the support flanges. Handle panels with care.

HOW TO INSTALL CEILING TILE

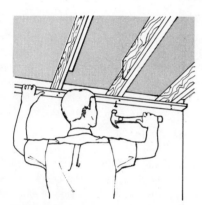

Nail first furring strip flush against wall at a right angle to ceiling joists, rest of strips parallel to the first one.

Space strips by width of one tile, using tile or tape to measure. Check with tape about every fourth strip to insure accuracy.

Check strips with carpenter's level; correct any high spots by driving cardboard or thin wood chips between strip and joist.

Start tile installation in a corner of ceiling. Face-nail tile to wall-edge furring strip and staple through exposed tile flanges.

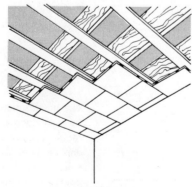

Work out from corner, installing about two border tiles at a time along each wall and then filling in with more tiles.

To install tiles directly on ceiling, daub adhesive in corners and center of tile backs. Press tile in place and, if required, staple.

the string at the reference corner. Install the other main grid supports in the same way, exactly parallel to the preceding one and separated from it by precisely the panel dimension used in the computation—not the odd support-to-wall dimension used to locate the first support.

Cross grid supports may have to be modified to fit odd dimensions of perimeter panels, depending on the system used. Install the first cross supports in line with the right-angled string, all others parallel to the preceding one and spaced from it by precisely the panel measurement used in computations. Most ready-made grids provide accurate standard spacing of cross grids automatically.

Drop standard panels into their grid sections. If the walls are wavy, out of plumb, or at odd angles to each other, individual trimming may be necessary for the odd-sized panels around the perimeter.

CEILING TILE

Standard square or rectangular ceiling tile can be mounted with adhesive or staples either directly on existing ceilings that are clean and sound or on furring strips applied to the old ceiling. Estimate the number of tiles needed and the dimensions of the odd-sized perimeter tiles by the same methods as for suspended-ceiling paneling—just substitute "tile" wherever "panel" is mentioned.

Installation on Furring Strips

Apply 1 by 4-inch furring strips at right angles to the ceiling joints by the same string layout methods described for suspended ceiling grid supports. There should be furring strips at all wall-to-ceiling junctions (don't include these in computations). The centerline of the second strip will be spaced from the wall edge by the distance of the perimeter tile dimension. Space the succeeding furring strip center-lines exactly on the tile width dimensions from the preceding strip centerline (see sketch below).

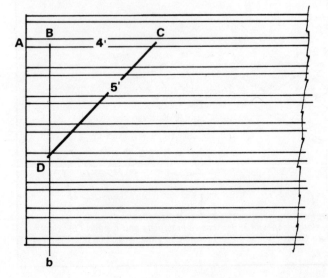

Keep all furring strips at the same level by using wood or cardboard shims between strips and joists where needed.

Start stapling at the reference corner. Cut tiles where they abut the wall, and nail through the face of the tile to the wall edge furring strip. The grooved edge of the tile should exactly reach the center of the adjoining furring strip. Staple exposed stapling flange to strip, then snuggly fit and staple adjoining tiles. Remember to work tongued edges toward reference walls.

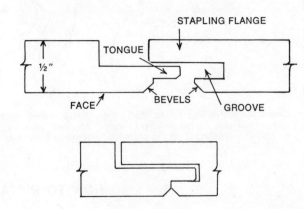

Work out from corner, mounting two or three perimeter strip tiles along each wall, joining with standard tiles, and repeating the process until the entire ceiling is covered. Perimeter tiles with grooved edges removed and fitted to the wall should be face-nailed to the wall edge furring strip.

Direct-to-Ceiling Installation

Apply the recommended adhesive, in dabs about the diameter and thicknesses of a half dollar, in the center and an inch or two from each corner on the back side of each tile. Press the tile firmly in place.

Some adhesives require use of one or two staples through strapling flanges to hold tile until adhesive dries.

The same computations, layout, and general installation instructions apply as for tile stapled to furring strips, except that with some adhesives face nailing at wall edges may not be necessary.

DRY-WALL GYPSUM CEILING PANELS

The homeowner can install dry-wall "plaster" ceilings, but he will seldom find it worth the trouble. This kind of ceiling requires heavy lifting, is easily damaged during installation, and requires taping, spackling, smoothing, and sizing for smooth surfaces or, at best, application of heavily textured coatings to hide defects. When it's all done, it isn't noticeably less expensive than an attractive suspended-panel ceiling.

If it seems absolutely necessary to have plastered or dry-wall panel ceilings, have a professional do the job or refer to books available on the subject.

Suspended garage ceiling *has metal beams, and 2 by 4-foot acoustical softboard panels. The tile dampens the sound of power tools, reflects light well, and helps insulate in summer and winter.*

Translucent plastic panels *placed in suspended ceiling give closed-in bathroom bright and cheery lighting.*

Fissured acoustical tile *reflects cove lighting, absorbs sound in this high-ceilinged living-dining area.*

Bringing in more daylight

Architects and designers have been devoting a good deal of time and effort toward designing effective ways of bringing daylight into the house. One of the earliest developments was the sliding glass door. The so-called picture window continued to grow larger; and windows in general increased in number and in size. Clerestories were used to let daylight in above standard ceiling heights. Ribbon windows filled end walls and stairwells to wash walls with light and offer outside views.

Then, with house walls well opened up, architects began to see new possibilities—skylights could pierce the roof and bring overhead daylight into interior spaces for special effects. The latest trend toward achieving greater daylight in the house has been the use of sky windows—a kind of mixture of skylight, window wall, and clerestory.

Following is a discussion of the advantages and effectiveness of each of these approaches to increased daylight.

THE TWO-STORY WINDOW WALL

Use of a two-story glass wall has the effect of enlarging the interior. It can also help to fit a hillside house to its site and view, give a box-shaped house character inside and out, and open up a cabin to the grandeur of a mountain setting. Two-story glass can dramatically open both high-ceilinged living areas and interior balcony space to the outdoors, for effects far more interesting than a single-level ceiling allows.

Consider the Need for Privacy. Privacy is not a major factor with a mountain cabin, a house on a hillside, or a house in dense woods. However, in the usual city residence, a window wall may require a low balcony wall or row of cabinets for a privacy screen. Another way to achieve privacy from the street is to use two-story draperies.

Consider Your Heating System. Your heating system must cope with considerable heat loss through the glass, and drafts from the upper floor. With a warm-air system, place registers at the foot of the window wall. This will offset the coldness next to the glass with a curtain of warm air.

Consider the Need for Sun Control. A south or west-facing window wall is often hard to shade against the afternoon sun. If your view faces the afternoon sun, you must decide between two-story glass and coolness inside. In most cases sun can be controlled with draperies, blinds, or tinted glass.

THE USE OF SKYLIGHTS

For the remodeler, a skylight is perhaps the most practical way to get natural light into a room or hall where light has been blocked off by an addition that eliminates an existing window wall. It's often the easiest way to get more daylight into rooms in an older house instead of enlarging windows.

The Need for Privacy can also be an important factor in installing a skylight. In a house on a narrow lot, for example, with windows facing a neighbor's house, you may have to draw the curtains even during the day. A skylight will eliminate the perpetual gloom.

Legal Restrictions must be checked before installation of a skylight. Most cities have building regulations that apply to skylights, so before going ahead with your remodeling plans, check with the building inspector. Either glass or plastic is permitted in skylights, but you must use wire glass or a code-approved type of plastic. There are also code limits on how much area you can cover with each kind of skylight material. Other restrictions may include distance of the house from property line and spacing between skylight units.

Clear or Translucent? Clear skylights are wonderful if you want to look up at the clouds or at tall trees, and they admit about 85 to 92 per cent of available light. In many areas this may present no problem. In the desert and other regions of intense sunlight, however, you'll probably prefer a skylight of translucent plastic or glass.

The Skylight's Appearance. Usually anything that protrudes above the surface of a roof can be seen from the street. A skylight, because of its size, is pretty difficult to hide if the roof slopes. Manufacturers are well aware of this and have designed models as low in silhouette as possible, and in various styles to adapt to various types of roofs.

THE SKY-TURNED WINDOW

Sometimes, the sky window takes the form of a window wall extension angling up above the eave line and becoming a part of the roof itself. At other times it may be a large, high-up window for a view of trees or sky, replacing the normal ceiling. Whether it's legally a skylight or a window depends on its location in the house and the interpretation of applicable building code requirements.

If Classified as a Skylight, the opening can have clear plastic or a wired glass. Restrictions are mainly to insure the safety of persons on the roof who might walk or fall into a skylight, and to protect those inside against breaking glass. If the opening is used solely as a source of light, you could use wired glass in one of many patterns, or a clear or translucent plastic skylight. If the opening faces north, clear wired glass is suitable since the window won't get direct sun. But for an eastern or western exposure, and to a lesser degree for a southern one, sun and glare can be a problem.

If Classified as a Window, the opening can be covered with one of a wide choice of glass types for almost any daylight condition. There are tinted and heat-absorbing glasses to reduce glare and cut down heat buildup inside the house. Insulating glass will reduce heat buildup in the summer and heat loss in winter. (For more details on types and selections of glass, see pages 122-123.)

THE CLERESTORY WINDOW

Whereas a skylight or sky window generally is an opening in a roof, a clerestory is a vertical opening in a wall plane that goes above the normal ceiling height. In many ways the clerestory window gives the best demonstration of the benefits of daylighting from high overhead.

Clerestories Normally Require a Lofty Ceiling, usually a change in ceiling level, and tend to create an interesting variety of interior space. By throwing light into the center of the interior space, they somewhat relax the restrictions on where windows and other elements of the house and its furnishings may be placed. Clerestories draw your eye out of its accustomed horizontal path to explore upward.

Fewer Direct Sun Problems are encountered with the use of clerestories than with skylights. The windows can be sheltered under a roof overhang, or the direct sun confined to a comparatively small aperture. And if the clerestories are made to open, ventilation can be greatly improved.

Clear plastic skylight in master bedroom roof is 6 by 6 feet, gives splendid view of stars at night.

Clerestory windows admit daylight to otherwise closed-in living room, have colorful stained glass panels.

Two-story glass wall overlooks interior court, contributes to apparent size of living-dining area below, bedroom above.

High windows are slanted to face sky and view of trees, are glazed with tinted glass to reduce inside glare.

Wide source lighting

The wide light source (developed during the years following World War II) is still the most popular approach to home lighting. One reason for this continued popularity has been the continuous improvement of fluorescent tubes and experiments that show what a pleasing effect you get when you give a house widely spread, well diffused light.

What is a Wide Light Source?

Perhaps the most meaningful explanation of a wide light source is to say that it is an extended area of light. It starts with a fluorescent or filament tube or a group of bulbs as a light source. From there it can become an expansion of the familiar recessed ceiling panel into a 4-foot square of light, or into a sizable area of luminous ceiling. Sometimes it is a diffusing skylight equipped to give both day and night lighting.

Or it may be no more than a light bulb surrounded by a luminous sphere, cylinder, or cube. Sometimes its main element is a diffusing material that gathers the light from bulbs or tubes set behind it. This can take the form of a shoji or a translucent room divider panel made luminous with light thrown on it from above or to the side.

Extended area lighting is not the whole answer to home lighting, of course, but it has proven itself as possibly the best approach to the whole complex of factors that affect lighting.

Why Widen the Source of Light?

Extending a source of light helps to solve two main problems in lighting: how to get enough well distributed light, and how to prevent glare. By widening the source, you can provide more light without increasing brightness, which in turn produces glare when it is excessive.

Three single 50-watt bulbs give about as much light as one 150-watt bulb, but their brightness is spread out so that at any one of the smaller sources, the brightness is only ⅓ that of the larger. The long fluorescent tube offers a convenient way of applying this spreading-out principle.

Of course, you have to do more than widen the source, if you want to keep glare to a minimum. Here are some other things you should do:

Shield the Source and place it where it is unobtrusive. It is distracting if you are more aware of the light source than of the light it gives. A recessed light ceiling panel doesn't bother most people, simply because they seldom look up, even though the light source is quite visible. But many other sources need either concealment or shielding.

Diffuse the Light. This can be done with a variety of translucent materials—glass, plastic, or fabric. Egg-crate and honeycomb grille arrangements are devices primarily for shielding the source of light, but while they pass direct light downward, they also act as good means to diffuse light to the side by reflection from the many surfaces of the grille. In indirect lighting, light is diffused by reflection from walls or ceiling.

Reduce Light Contrasts. The eye has to strain and becomes fatigued when adjusting simultaneously to light and dark, as when you look at a brightly lighted book page or a glowing television screen in a dark room. To overcome this contrast, you can raise the amount of general light in a room, by installing additional fixtures, not brighter bulbs.

What About Reflection?

You can use reflection to diffuse light and to control the actual amount of light. Wall, ceiling, and floor surfaces are useful elements in many schemes for wide source lighting.

Dull mat surfaces reflect a pleasing diffused light that is generally without glare; shiny surfaces reflect without much diffusion and often produce glare. Light colored surfaces reflect more light than dark surfaces. A white wall reflects about 75 per cent of the light; a black wall, about 10 per cent.

Some wood interiors can be bleached or given a light wash of paint to improve their reflective qualities without hiding the grain. However, if you have such light-swallowing surfaces as a bookshelf wall or rich colored redwood walls that you don't want to refinish, the only way to attack the problem is to add enough light to overcome the lack of reflection.

Incandescent or Fluorescent Light?

Incandescent bulbs and tubes give off a yellow light. This is the color of artificial light that pleases most people, because they are used to it, and because it flatters human coloring. However, it tends to subdue the blues and greens of materials. The pink bulb casts a warm, cozy glow, but at the expense of the cool colors.

Deluxe colors in fluorescent tubes made them more suitable for home lighting. Unlike the standard fluorescent colors, these have good color rendition and are more flattering to human coloring. Use the deluxe' warm white tubes for a predominately warm color scheme, or the deluxe cool white where cool colors predominate in a room and where you want a fresh, cool effect.

There is now a new light on the market which combines the best qualities of incandescent and fluorescent lighting. The lighting tubes are covered with a newly developed phosphor which allows for warm, but bright and long-lasting illumination.

SIX WAYS TO BUILD IN WIDE SOURCE LIGHTING

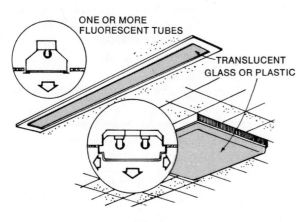

The ceiling troffer. *These "light boxes" in the ceiling should be wide-area for shadowless general light, low-brightness for comfort. Use more fixtures for a given amount of light rather than put more tubes in one troffer.*

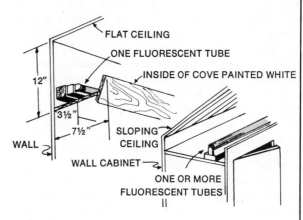

The cove. *Indirect light on mat surface, about one-half as efficient as most wall lighting. Cove distance from ceiling is usually 1/10 width of room, but cove should be at least 12 inches below flat ceiling. Monotonous if used alone.*

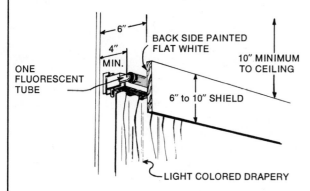

The lighted valance. *A natural place for linear light; for both up and down light, should be at least 10 inches below flat ceiling—otherwise shield the top. Lamp should be at least 4 inches out from wall and beyond draperies.*

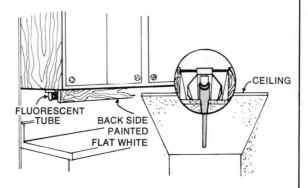

The ribbon of light. *Used with or without shield or diffuser. For use as down light, it is generally mounted in a soffit. Sometimes built in as extended "pin-hole" source to light a passageway or to define a room area.*

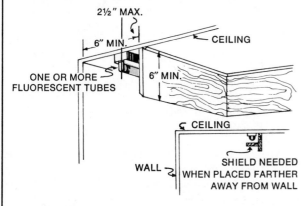

The lighted cornice. *Often extends the length of a wall. Place farther out from wall and use horizontal shield for a more dramatic, effective bath of light. Be careful of too great a contrast with a dark ceiling.*

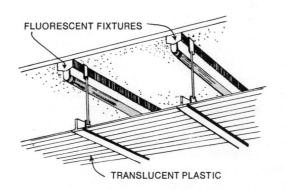

The luminous ceiling. *Extension of troffer principle to entire ceiling. Good for critical light; for general light should have brightness control. Expense of extra ceiling is offset by reduced finishing cost.*

Noise...what to do about it

Too many of today's houses are too noisy. And as houses become more tightly organized, with more machines and gadgets as potential noise makers, the need for sound control will be even greater.

Many sound-proofing materials developed for commercial buildings are available to the home owner and will suffice for relatively minor sound problems. But for a major sound problem, it is best to seek out a special consultant.

If you are sensitive to noise you can be plagued in three different ways:

1. You may find the sounds which originate within a room too loud, or reverberant.

2. You may be disturbed by noises which originate in other parts of the house—in rooms on either side of you or, in a multi-level house, from the rooms above or below.

3. You may be disturbed by noises which originate outside the house.

If you have any one of these sound problems, the discussion below and on the next page will help you to analyze it and also will suggest what you might do about it.

When Noise Originates Within a Room

There are two ways to deal with noise originating within a room. You can eliminate it entirely, or you can absorb part of it.

Eliminating noise is, of course, the most obvious approach. Place vibrating appliances on rubber pads. Oil squeaky motors. Use mechanical door closers or buffers to prevent slamming doors. A few such solutions may add up to a surprisingly quieter house.

There is a limit to how much noise that can be eliminated, however, and some rooms—even with relatively little sound originating in them—still seem noisy. Echoes are caused by sounds bouncing off hard, reflective surfaces and coming at the ear from several directions. When someone speaks in an empty room, for example, you hear the spoken word as the sound comes from his mouth. Then, a split-second later, you hear it again; or you hear part of it as it reflects off walls, ceiling, or floor.

Use Soft, Porous Absorptive Surfaces to dampen echoes. In a living room, it is easy to add enough rugs or carpets, upholstered furniture, or heavy curtains to bring sound down to a satisfactory level. Be careful not to absorb too much sound, however, or the room will take on a dead quality.

Use Acoustical Tiles on the ceilings of particularly noisy rooms such as the kitchen, a family room, or a recreation room. These tiles—like other soft building boards—are made variously of wood, cane, or mineral fibers pressed and cut into different sizes. Some tiles are perforated with many small holes which trap rather than reflect sound striking them, thereby lowering the noise level. Other tiles have porous, textured surfaces. (See the step-by-step guide for installing ceiling tiles on page 111.)

When Noise Originates in Other Parts of the House

You may find it more difficult to stop noise entering a room from another part of the house. First, you must determine how the sound enters (through the floor or ceiling, through a wall, through or around windows, along floor joists). Realize that sound travels most easily through lightweight materials and enters through small openings almost as well as through big ones.

If Sound Travels Through Walls, do not think that a sound absorbing surface on a wall of a room will prevent all sound from traveling to the next room. Insulation is usually the best way to keep sound from going through walls. The heavier the insulation, the more effective it is, but materials that are generally good sound absorbers (within a room) are poor sound insulators (between rooms). See the sketches on the next page showing the difference between absorbing sound and insulating against it.

Where it is not practical to insulate, you can *isolate* one room from another by separating them with walls which do not share common studs.

In one wall you might put two rows of studs so that sound striking one wall cannot travel through the stud to the next wall (see sketch below).

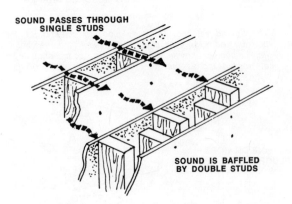

SOUND PASSES THROUGH SINGLE STUDS

SOUND IS BAFFLED BY DOUBLE STUDS

You can also use two or three thicknesses of gypsum board (see sketch at top of next page) or one of the newer sound-deadening wall panelings to prevent sound from traveling through walls. This same treatment may work on a ceiling to keep sound from traveling to an upstairs room or from an upstairs room down to you.

If Sound is Traveling Through a Door, first determine how much is actually coming through the door, and how much

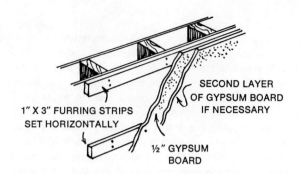

1" X 3" FURRING STRIPS
SET HORIZONTALLY

SECOND LAYER
OF GYPSUM BOARD
IF NECESSARY

½" GYPSUM
BOARD

under. To test, stuff a piece of heavy felt pad at the bottom or around the edges. If this brings the sound level down to a tolerable point, weatherstrip the perimeter of the door with heavy felt or strips of sponge rubber.

If too much sound still comes through a hollow core door, you'll find a slab door more effective.

When Noise Comes from Outside the House

When noise enters from outside the house, first check to see whether or not it is coming through open windows. If it is, you may find it feasible to keep all windows on the noisy side closed and do your venting entirely on the quiet side of the house. If the noise level is disturbing even through a closed window, you might consider double insulating glass.

When Noise Comes Through the Plumbing

Plumbing noises are often caused by vibrations set up when water runs through pipes.

Decrease Vibration by using large-diameter pipes. The same amount of water will travel through a one-inch pipe at a lower velocity and vibrate less than in a ¾-inch pipe.

Dampen Vibration by padding direct connections between pipes and structure with heavy felt. When pipes have to be suspended, as from the floor joists in the crawl space under the house, suspend them with limp wire rather than with stiff rods. It will allow the pipes to vibrate freely without transmitting the vibrations to the joist.

Minimize the Sound of Water. For an outdoor sprinkling system, you will need a separate line for the out-of-doors, completely detached from the house system. This will mean the extra expense of buying additional pipe, and paying for labor to dig the ditches all around the house.

The best way to avoid the flushing noise of a toilet is to buy one of the cast, one-piece units specially designed to flush almost noiselessly. They are, of course, considerably more expensive than standard toilets.

Sound is Not Simple

Although a home owner can do much to bring the noise level down, using the principles and ideas suggested above, sound control problems are often too complex for the layman to analyze, working without technical training, experience, or benefit of instruments.

Sound behaves differently at different frequencies. High tones are more or less directional, and they can be blocked or deflected more easily than low tones. In practical terms, this means that it is easier to create a soundproof room for a flute player than for a tuba player.

Before embarking on any remodeling to control sound, beyond the simple suggestions made here, be sure to consult with an architect, contractor, or building materials supply store about the latest products and methods for installing sound deadening devices.

KEEPING SOUND WHERE IT BELONGS

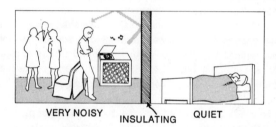

VERY NOISY   INSULATING   QUIET

Dense insulating wall, such as masonry, between two rooms, prevents sound from traveling from one room to another, but allows the sound to reverberate greatly in one room.

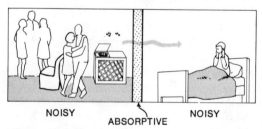

NOISY   ABSORPTIVE   NOISY

Absorptive material between rooms eliminates some reverberation in a noisy room, but also allows sound to travel through the wall. Sound also travels through heating ducts.

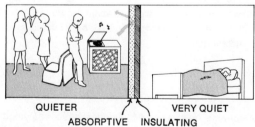

QUIETER   ABSORPTIVE   INSULATING   VERY QUIET

Combination of absorptive and insulating material between rooms controls noise reverberation in one room and at the same time stops sound from traveling to the next room.

Installing wall panelings

Paneling is probably the fastest to install of any of the low-upkeep wall coverings. Its wide range of colors, protective finishes, and textures offer the homeowner many ways to add beauty and utility to otherwise drab walls.

ASSEMBLING THE MATERIALS

Before buying materials to panel a wall, you must decide on the overall effect you want to achieve. You may want broad, uninterrupted expanses of color, pattern, or texture; a grooved or planked surface; or color, pattern, and texture contrasts provided by alternating panels, dividers, or spacing.

Select the paneling size best suited to producing the desired effect. Materials available range from planks as narrow as 3 inches through panels 16 and 48 inches wide to odd-sized pieces such as parquet flooring and roofing shingles. Pick the paneling material itself on the basis of visual effect, durability, and cost.

Next choose the surface finish. Unfinished paneling is least expensive and allows the creation of special finishes, but pre-finished panels save much time and effort and probably are a better buy for the homeowner. Special finishes which resist water, abrasion, and impact are available.

Decide on the wall mounting method to be used. This often is influenced, if not dictated, by the choice of paneling material. Methods include all-nail installation, which often is time-consuming and mars the surface; and combined nailing and gluing with panel adhesives. Special clips are designed for use with some panels.

WHEN YOU BUY THE PANELING

Dealers' stocks usually are represented by stacks or racks of samples, but try to hand select your own panels for good pattern and color match. No dealer can be expected to have every color, texture, or material in stock or sample, but many can order special items, including matching or contrasting moldings to finish off the paneling edges.

Try to have the paneling delivered several days ahead of when you plan to install it. Stack it in the area to be paneled to allow it to acclimate itself to temperature and humidity conditions, thus preventing warping and buckling problems after installation.

ESTIMATE THE MATERIALS REQUIRED

To determine how many 4-foot-wide panels you need per wall, measure the length of the wall in feet and divide by 4. Round fractions off to the next largest number. For materials like planking or shingles the dealer should have tables with which he can compute the amount of material you need. Use his computation, with the understanding—written on the receipt—that all undamaged and uncut materials can be returned for refund or credit. Door and window areas may be deducted, but remember that it is much easier to cut out areas from whole sheets than to try to do a blemish-free fitting and piecing job at or below eye level.

If a wall is more than 8 feet tall, order extra-long panels, or allow for extra panels to piece out the height. Balance the proportionately greater cost of nonstandard panel lengths against the work required to cut and piece additional height—this can be fairly easy if picture molding is used to hide irregularities between the panels. On the other hand, you might consider using the decorator's ceiling-lowering trick, capping the paneling with molding at 8 feet and painting the exposed wall to match the ceiling.

Nails, clips, glue, and molding purchases will depend on the mounting method used.

PREPARING THE WALL

If the wall is clean, level, smooth, and moisture-free, paneling can be applied with adhesives directly to the surface so long as there are subsurface wooden wall members (studs, plates, sills) to which it can be end-nailed. Rough or damaged surfaces can be repaired with commercial patching compounds if other conditions are met.

On the other hand, if the wall surface is dirty, flaking, moist, or too rough to repair, or if it needs insulation, furring strips must be used. Lack of suitably spaced subsurface wooden wall members for nailing may necessitate use of furring, as may special materials such as shingles or panels narrower than 16 inches (normal stud spacing) which might require mid-panel nailing.

Furring strips, usually 1 by 3-inch or 2 by 2-inch wooden strips, are attached to the wall to provide good nailing or gluing surfaces. They most often are spaced 16 inches apart at right angles to the wall studs. For use with adhesives on narrow horizontal paneling, furring strips are attached vertically and directly over the studs.

A common practice where minimal help is needed for nailing and gluing is the use of plywood furring strips 3 inches wide but only ¼ or ⅜ inch thick, especially where thicker strips would create too much bulk.

MOUNTING THE PANELING

Mounting methods are virtually identical for furred and unfurred walls. The only difference is that furring strips dictate glue, nail, and clip placement on the strips, while unfurred walls require nail and clip placement over weight-supporting members (such as studs, lintels, plates, sills, or masonry) but allow random mid-panel placement of adhesives.

All-Nail Mounting

This method calls for nailing through wide panels, as inconspicuously as possible, into wall-supporting members or furring strips. Wherever possible, use color-matched nails and drive them into textured areas such as grooves, which most manufacturers conveniently locate on 16-inch stud and furring centers, or through the tongues of tongue-and-groove boards.

If visible nail heads are objectionable, recess them with a nail set. Use a color-matched puttying or repair stick to blend the surface.

Nail-and-Adhesive Mounting

To mount butt or lap joint panels this way, apply adhesive in squiggly stripes to all furring or exposed wall, studs, plates, lintels, and sills. Press the panel into position, then drive two or more finishing nails through one end of the panel partway into the wall to act as locating and hinge pins. Pull the bottom edge of the panel about 6 inches out from the wall to allow adhesive to partially air-cure.

After 10 minutes or so, firmly press the panel back into place and use a rubber mallet or hammer on a padded block to force the adhesive into tight contact. Drive the hinge pin nails all the way in, and nail the panel along its top and bottom edges to the wall.

Adhesive works best on direct-to-the-wall applications when applied in uniformly spaced stripes 12 to 16 inches apart. All thin paneling materials require either a glue stripe or nailing within a half inch of panel edges to prevent curling or lipping.

Skip the hinge pin nailing on lock or tongue-and-groove jointed panel materials, since it would interfere with panel application. All other operations do apply, including nailing both ends after final adhesive installation. Nailing can be done through the tongue of tongue-and-groove panels to hide nail heads.

Clip-and-Adhesive Mounting

Almost identical to nail-and-adhesive applications, this method can be used with some tongue-and-groove panels. Instead of hinge pin nailing, clips are nailed to wall or furring strips as locators for the panels. The adhesive is applied the same as for nail-and-adhesive mounting.

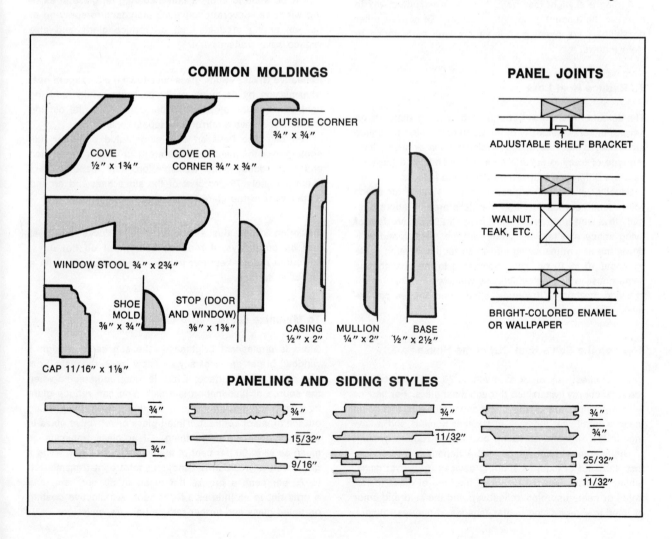

COMMON MOLDINGS

COVE ½″ x 1¾″

COVE OR CORNER ¾″ x ¾″

OUTSIDE CORNER ¾″ x ¾″

WINDOW STOOL ¾″ x 2¾″

SHOE MOLD ⅜″ x ¾″

STOP (DOOR AND WINDOW) ⅜″ x 1⅜″

CASING ½″ x 2″

MULLION ¼″ x 2″

BASE ½″ x 2½″

CAP 11/16″ x 1⅛″

PANEL JOINTS

ADJUSTABLE SHELF BRACKET

WALNUT, TEAK, ETC.

BRIGHT-COLORED ENAMEL OR WALLPAPER

PANELING AND SIDING STYLES

¾″   ¾″   ¾″   ¾″

¾″   15/32″   11/32″   ¾″

9/16″   25/32″

11/32″

What you need to know about glass

Most home owners have little reason to think much about glass. It lets in light, opens up a view, must be cleaned now and then—and is accepted on that basis.

But when you're in the process of remodeling, knowing a bit more about glass can be of considerable benefit. There are a great many kinds of glass to choose from for windows, walls, and doors; each has its purpose, advantages, and cost factors. The information on these two pages will help you to take fuller advantage of this variety to make your house more comfortable in the summer, warmer in the winter, and safer the year around.

To Increase the Amount of Daylight Entering a Room

First, use clear glass. Outside, use highly reflective materials: light-colored paving, grayish or whitish plant material. Paint the underside of overhangs in a highly reflective color. Inside, paint the room in a light color and use bright fabrics and light floors.

Adding a skylight (see page 114) is an excellent way to increase the amount of daylight in a room. Of course, other possibilities are opening up the room with clerestories or sky windows.

To Reduce Heat Loss

The amount of heat lost through window areas depends on several factors: the ability of the weatherstripping to reduce air leakage, the kind of glass (single pane or insulating), the type of framing material (metal or wood), and the temperature difference between outdoors and indoors.

Usually, an insulating glass unit with ½-inch air space will reduce heat loss through the glass area by about one-half. In a well built house with about 1,200 square feet of living space and ten well made and weatherstripped windows, the use of insulating glass can reduce heating costs by about 10 to 15 per cent, compared to the cost for the same house with single-thickness windows.

Inside the house, draperies, blinds, and shades can reduce heat loss.

To Keep the Sun's Heat Out of the House

You can effectively block as much as 70 to 80 per cent of the solar energy transmitted through clear glass. For houses with large glass areas on the east and west walls, this could mean a significant increase in summer comfort and a savings in the size and operating cost of the cooling system.

The amount of heat you can block depends on three factors: the kind of external shading devices (roof overhangs, fences, trellises, special screens); the kind of glass (clear, tinted or heat-absorbing, reflective); and the kind and color of interior sun-blocking matter (shades, draperies, blinds).

In planning solar heat control, remember that summer heat gain is greatest in the early morning and late afternoon when the sun is relatively low in the sky; therefore east and west sides of the house receive the most solar energy. Architectural projections and screens should be designed with this in mind.

Tinted Glass, Heat-Absorbing Glass. Such glass can block much solar radiation—although part of it is soon reradiated to the inside as heat.

How much does tinted glass alter colors? From within, gray provides very natural color retention. Bronze may make the outdoors appear slightly brighter while actually reducing light intensity; but most people observing the outdoors through it will be unaware of any change in color. Green slightly intensifies green colors and tends to make the outdoors seem cooler. Generally, the color is chosen less for its effect on visibility and more for the tone it imparts to the building's exterior.

It is possible to apply a tinted coating on glass in existing windows. Several companies manufacture spray-on or flow-on tinting products that do reduce glare, and also reduce solar transmission.

Reflective Glass. Such glass cuts down the amount of heat transmission by as much as 70 per cent, while reducing light transmission by 50 to 70 per cent. From the outside the windows have a mirror-like appearance.

You can also have an aluminum-coated polyester film applied over the inside of glass areas to increase reflection and thus reduce solar transmission. The manufacturers claim it rejects 75 per cent of the sun's heat and around 80 per cent of the glare.

Insulating Glass. Just as insulating glass blocks some heat loss on cold days, it reduces heat input on hot days. To further reduce heat transmission, order the glass with a reflective surface.

To Minimize Glare

Glare is unpleasant brightness—the sun seen through a window, bright areas of sky or snow, reflected light from water or a shiny surface. Glare is most bothersome when the source of illumination is small. You can reduce glare by controlling the intensity of the brightness, by evening out the areas of contrast. Tinted glass or reflective glass in windows does the same thing. Clear glass transmits as much as 88 to 90 per cent of the available daylight, while a glass with a greenish tint may cut total light transmission to 75 per cent, a bronze tint to about 50 per cent, and a gray tint to as little as 14 per cent. A reflective coating on tinted glass can further reduce light transmission.

To Reduce Condensation

Sometimes you can reduce condensation that interferes with your enjoyment of a particular view by replacing the existing glass with insulating glass. By keeping indoor glass surfaces warmer on cold days, you can permit indoor humidity levels to go quite high without causing condensation.

New insulating glass products with a special reflective coating insulates like three sheets of glass and therefore permits still higher winter indoor humidity before condensation occurs.

To Provide Privacy

Where good light is required yet privacy is important, use patterned glass. The degree of obscurity is determined by the pattern you choose. Patterned glass is desirable for its light-diffusing properties. If safety is a factor, use tempered or wired patterned glass. It's also available with a glare-reducing finish.

Where through-vision is needed or desired, tinted glass and reflective glass provide some degree of privacy during the day with little impairment of the view to the outside.

To Provide Maximum Safety and Security

Building codes in most areas now require tempered, wired, or laminated glass in all glazed areas that may be mistaken for an opening and that extend to within 18 inches of the floor unless there are push bars or permanent protective screens.

Tempered Glass should be used in fixed and sliding patio windows and doors, in shower and tub enclosures, and wherever people may mistake the glass for an opening or bump into it for other reasons.

Wired Glass is widely used in skylights, shower doors, wind screens, and other places where safety is a major factor. The glass itself is no stronger than the unwired ordinary kind, but the wire offers a measure of resistance to penetration and helps hold the glass together in the event of breakage.

To Reduce Sound

Glass can reduce sound transmission, muffling the noises of trains, traffic, and children playing. Thicker glass is more effective than thinner glass. You can even buy special sound-control glass that has thick plastic layers laminated between two sheets of glass.

But the amount of reduction is partly dependent on the amount of sound leakage in the window frame; and sound can also leak around and through doors and through the house walls themselves. Airtight resilient weatherstripping around all openings will help.

HOW TO REPLACE A WINDOW PANE

FOR A WOODEN SASH, putty or glazing compound is usually used to seal and hold the glass against the sash seat. Slip-on U-shaped rubber molding or glazing compound is sometimes used as a sealer behind replaceable wooden retainer strips.

METAL SASHES are either of single-unit construction similar to wood sashes, designed for press-fit molded rubber or plastic retainer strips, or have one or more removable sides to allow for glass installation into blind grooves. The sash is a single-unit type if around the indoor-facing edge of the glass there is a fairly wide rubber molding, which can be easily pried out at a corner and stripped free. If the glass sealing material is very thin, look to the sash corners for clips, retainers and springs, screws, or rivets which may be in the sash face or on the narrow edges. Flat, metal, corner-straddling clips—often hidden in recesses in the narrow edges—can be gently pried loose with a thin blade or screwdriver. L-shaped retainers with wire clips, and often sashes with no other visible means of disassembly, usually indicate a knock-down sash. Lay a smooth wooden block on the glass and against the top sash edge and use firm hammer taps to push the top sash rail free of the side rails.

Screws should be removed with care so that internal corner braces won't fall free before their position can be seen. Sometimes only one or two screws on each corner need be removed. Rivets have to be drilled out and replaced by screws or new rivets. Determine whether internal bracing or screw or rivet positions require corner shaping of new glass.

INSTALLING GLASS

CUT GLASS SLIGHTLY undersize in both width and height to allow for expansion and contraction. A wood sash requires ⅛-inch undersizing. A metal sash requires 1/16-inch undersizing.

MOLDED U-CHANNEL SEALING STRIPS used on some sashes seldom require use of glazing compound, but a rubber lubricant may be needed to facilitate sliding the strip onto the glass and into the sash channels.

GLAZING COMPOUND should be used to seal and to cushion where sealer-cushion strips are not provided. Apply a 1/16-inch layer of compound to the lips of the glass seat before installing glass. Install any retaining clips or springs provided for metal sashes, or glazing points for wooden sashes. If replaceable wooden or metal strips are used to retain the glass, apply a layer of compound to their glass-contact surfaces before installing.

GLAZING COMPOUND, when used as the prime glass retainer, must be applied in a smooth, continuous strip sloping up from the outer seat edge to the glass surface to match the height of the backup retaining lip, which is seldom less than ⅜-inch high. A pencil-thick strip of compound can be applied with a narrow putty knife, a spatula, or your thumb.

Installing floor coverings

If a messy and back-breaking experience laying a floor covering years ago has kept you from attempting it again, you may be pleasantly surprised by some of the kinds of resilient floor surfaces on the market today. New developments stress simplified installation and provide choices specifically designed to fit almost any situation. There are seamless plastic roll-on floors, self-adhering tiles, and sheet flooring you apply without adhesives. There is flooring designed to withstand outdoor use. And a wealth of patterns includes photographic impressions of brick and tile, wood grain and pebble designs, and game-board insets for recreation rooms.

With such a wide range of floor coverings to choose from, laying a floor now more than ever, is one of the home-improvement jobs in which a careful amateur can achieve professional-looking results.

NARROWING THE CHOICE

Your choice of material will depend on its cost, your existing floor, personal preference as to pattern and construction features, the use to be made of the floor, and whether or not you will do the job yourself. If your floor is below-grade or on-grade concrete, your choice usually is limited to asphalt, vinyl asbestos, or outdoor vinyl tiles. You may be able to use other types for an on-grade concrete floor with good waterproofing membrane and drainage. Choices for floors of wood, ceramic tile, or above-grade concrete with air space beneath include asphalt, vinyl asbestos, homogeneous vinyl, linoleum, rubber, rubber plastic, or cork.

A sheet flooring with vinyl surface, latex cushion center layer, and felt backing goes over older floors without gluing. Installation is also simple for a vinyl-asbestos tile with a pressure-adhesive backing; you peel a paper from the back, lay the tile in place, and walk on it.

Among fairly recent developments are seamless liquid-application floor coverings for both outdoors and indoors. Over a coat of special sealer, you roll on clear polyurethane and sprinkle on colored vinyl chips, roll them flat, and sand lightly. Then you roll on more polyurethane.

ASSEMBLING THE MATERIALS

To figure the number of tiles you need, measure the length and width of the room in inches; divide each figure by the tile width (usually 6 or 9 inches), increasing fractions to the nearest whole number; multiply the two resulting figures. For an irregularly-shaped room, figure each offset section separately. It's wise to add 2 or 4 per cent for wastage.

For most types of tiles you will need an adhesive spreader (toothed strip of metal or cardboard about 5 by 12 inches), a linoleum knife or tile cutter, a chalkline, a linoleum roller, a yardstick, and a carpenter's square. Floor covering stores rent tile cutters and linoleum rollers. You can also rent a floor sander, needed for old floors and some new ones. To remove old tile, you'll want a scraper and a blowtorch.

Get the adhesive recommended for the tile you are buying. Wood floors may require a crack filler or a layer of plywood, masonite, or particle board. For concrete you need a primer.

PREPARING THE FLOOR

Remove furniture and the baseboard molding. Prepare a smooth surface—irregularities will give an uneven tile surface. To achieve a good bond between tile and floor, remove all wax, paint, or varnish, and all oil or grease spots.

The Subfloor Must Be Smooth

All floor boards must be tight and all nails set. Plane ridges if necessary to achieve smooth surface, and fill cracks or slight hollows with crack filler. Sand thoroughly.

If the floor is too rough to prepare properly or if there is no subfloor, cover with a layer of plywood, masonite, or particle board. Nail with cement-coated, galvanized, or screw nails, to prevent "pop-up"; start from one corner or in the center of a panel—nailing the four corners first can make the panel springy.

The Concrete Floor—Apply Primer

If a concrete floor has been finished with wax, paint, or other substance, clean it with lacquer thinner (no smoking), then sand thoroughly. Apply a primer coat. Scrub well into the concrete.

Primer must dry for several hours, until all solvent odor has disappeared. Do not walk on the floor before it is dry. No lining material is used with concrete.

The Previously Tiled Floor—Clean or Remove

If the old tile is in quite good condition, you can lay new tile over it. (Some experts recommend removing old tile, regardless.) Remove all wax, and do not put new joints directly over joints in the old tile.

If the old tiling is not in good condition, you will need to remove it. Pull up all the tile, remove old adhesive with scraper and blowtorch, and sand with coarse sandpaper.

A filler which "floats" the floor can be used on old ceramic tile. It eliminates the need for sanding.

INSTALLING THE NEW FLOOR

You are ready to begin laying tiles after the entire subfloor is clean and smooth.

1. Make guide lines by connecting center points of opposite walls. Check crossed lines with a carpenter's square.

2. Lay a row of uncemented tile from the center point to one side wall and to one end wall. If the distance between the wall and the last tile is less than 2 inches or more than 8 inches, move the center line 4½ inches closer to the wall.

3. If you use quick-setting adhesive, spread only enough at a time for about 15 tiles. With slow-setting adhesive, spread an entire quarter section or more at once; allow it to become tacky before placing the tiles.

4. Set tiles in place; don't slide them, or you'll push adhesive up. (Immediately wipe off any adhesive that gets on the tile surface, using a damp cloth. Adhesive which has dried on the tile can be removed with fine steel wool and soapy water.) Press each tile down firmly, especially at the edges. Lay all whole tiles first.

Asphalt tile can be cut most easily if you heat the back with a blowtorch. Cut with tile cutter or tin snips. Score an unheated tile several times with a linoleum knife and snap in two. Other kinds can be cut with a tile cutter, knife, or scissors without heating. If tile ends in a doorway, lay halfway through, to end under a door if possible. Finish with a metal strip (over wood) or a beveled asphalt strip (over concrete).

5. To fit tile around pipes or other obstructions, make a paper pattern to fit exactly, trace onto tile, and cut.

6. You may want to use vinyl coving around the edges. Apply adhesive to the back and press against the wall.

Roll a floor of rubber, linoleum, or cork tiles. *Don't* roll asphalt or vinyl asbestos tile. If edges of asphalt tile appear raised, room warmth will flatten them in a few days.

Let the floor dry thoroughly—at least overnight. Then clean it, and wax or polish if you wish, before moving in furniture. Do not mop for at least a week.

HOW TO INSTALL FLOOR TILES

Establish guide lines by finding the center points of opposite walls, then connecting these points with chalk lines.

Place row of uncemented tile along chalk lines from the center point to one side wall, another row to the end wall.

Spread adhesive smoothly, being careful not to cover guide lines. Allow to become tacky before setting the tiles in place.

Set tiles in place without sliding them. Butt each tile against adjoining tiles. Remove any excess adhesive while still wet.

Trace patterns of pipe or other obstructions on paper, then trace outline onto tile. Cut with tile cutters, large scissors.

Use vinyl coving to complete floor installation. Cut pieces to proper lengths and fit into place. Let floor dry thoroughly.

How skillful is your painting?

The homeowner who plans to do the painting portion of a contracted remodeling project will find that he can save a good deal of money—money that can be put into extra detailing and special touches. Most people have acquired some skill at painting by the time they own a house, but have forgotten or have never learned many of the things a professional painter does automatically. The near-revolution in converting painting to a homeowner's skill that started with the appearance of the paint roller and easy-to-apply, water-thinned (latex) paints has advanced even further. The discussion below includes tips from experienced painters, to help keep your technical know-how abreast of the times.

WHAT'S NEW IN PAINTS?

Today, practically all interior paints are made up of synthetic resins or polymers in one form or another. The paint industry has put these synthetics to work in two distinct types of paint: water-thinned and solvent-thinned paint.

All-Purpose Exterior Paints

This new house paint is a water-mixed latex, a modified acrylic or vinyl emulsion that you can apply as easily as the popular latex masonry paints of the last few years.

Unlike those paints, which can be used only on masonry and stucco surfaces, this latex is for the entire exterior—wood, masonry, stucco, metal, asbestos, and composition board. Tests have proven that it has a long life and is highly resistant to blistering and sun facing. It dries to the touch in 20 minutes and can even be applied over damp wood.

Polyurethane Finishes

The new polyurethane clear finishes are oil-modified types and, with brush or spray gun, are as easy as varnish to apply. Besides being extremely durable, these finishes are resistant to breakdown caused by the ultra-violet rays of the sun.

Polyurethane products come in both satin and glossy clear finishes, and also in some colors of pigmented marine paint. You apply them in the same way as varnish, and use common mineral spirits for thinning and cleaning brushes. You can apply a polyurethane finish over old varnish of fair condition by sanding lightly to give a "tooth," and you can remove it with common paint remover.

Fire Resistant Paint

Interior flat wall paints are now available that contain an intumescent agent which bubbles up on contact with flame and acts as an insulation blanket between the painted surface and a fire. Approved by Underwriters' Laboratories, the paint is not fireproof but it does retard the spread of a fire, rather than feed the flames as most paint does. Unlike some similar paints of the past, the new are washable.

Rust Inhibitor Paint

On the store shelves today you will find several makes of enamels, metal primers, and clear finishes, in ordinary cans and in spray cans, that contain rust inhibitors. At least one is formulated especially for galvanized metal. The clear finishes in spray cans provide an easy way to protect such rust-prone equipment as window screens, door hardware, and light fixtures.

BRUSH OR ROLLER?—WHICH IS BEST?

Frequently it's best to use both. Experienced painters suggest using a roller on any flat surface with any paint, including the semi-gloss and gloss paints and enamels. For the latter, use either a used roller (with the lint worn out of the nap) or a short-nap, mohair-covered roller. These give a "pebbled" finish that is easy to brush out (you need a brush for most edge work anyway). First paint a large area with the roller. Then take the brush and work from the fresh edge inward—use a light touch in one direction only; reverse strokes might lift the paint. You'll find that this combination still works faster on a flat surface than using a brush alone.

You can buy rollers for many jobs—with long nap for rough surfaces, short nap for smooth surfaces, or narrow width for window frame and other detailing. An oversized roller for exterior painting with an inch-long nap will hold two to three times as much paint as an ordinary roller.

Brushes come in all sizes and shapes with nylon or hog bristles. For a small area, it's best to reserve a nylon brush for use with water-base paints, and a similar size of bristle or nylon brush for oil-base paints; don't use them interchangeably.

Among the special types of brushes you can buy are the following: *Flatting brushes,* 5 or 6 inches wide, for painting very large, flat surfaces; *Sash brushes,* 1½ to 2½ inches wide, with an angled head, for painting sash and trim quickly; *Round and oval brushes,* for varnishing and general painting.

How to Use a Roller

You should work slowly and smoothly with a roller (it will cover the area rapidly, regardless). Quick strokes result in splatters, and uneven pressure makes bubbles. You need not roll uniformly in one direction. In fact, the job will be better if you roll every which way.

Painters recommend that when applying flat wall paints with a roller you start each new strip a foot or two away and work back toward the wet edge of the last strip, lapping into it halfway. The resulting coat is more even.

How to Use a Brush

When painting with a brush, dip only about a third of the bristle into the paint. Take more and paint will load up in the heel and run down the handle. After dipping, most experts slap the brush gently against the side of the can to remove excess paint. You can also drag it lightly against the rim, although this is slower.

When using a quick-drying, water-mixed paint, first dip your brush in water and squeeze it out, and then start painting. The water helps prevent paint from getting into the heel of the brush and quickly hardening there.

On edged objects, such as shelves, you'll avoid dribbling if you brush out to the edge, rather than in from the edge. Similarly, let your brush strokes end at a groove or other indentation, rather than drag across it and "load" with paint.

WHERE TO START

Where you start painting can make considerable difference in the results. If you're ambitiously redoing a whole room, it is fairly obvious that you should start with the ceiling. But you also should start in a corner; and whether you're using a brush or a roller, you should start by painting a strip about 2 feet wide completely across the ceiling the shorter way. You will be returning sooner on the next strip, and so there will be less likelihood of lap marks. Paint each strip only as wide as you can reach comfortably (never more than 3 feet wide).

Next, paint the walls, which are easier. Simply start at a corner and continue around the room. Then comes the baseboard and window trim. Paint the doors last.

Wherever possible, start at the top and work down, whether you're painting a wall, a chair, or a boat. You will have fewer runs and spatters on fresh paint.

HOW TO CLEAN UP AFTER PAINTING

The dullest chore of painting is cleaning up afterwards, but in order to keep your brushes and rollers in good condition for the next painting project, they must be cleaned immediately after use. Also, any left-over paint must be stored properly in order to keep it from getting lumpy.

Cleaning a Brush

Whenever you are cleaning brushes you have used with water-mixed paint, add some detergent to the washing water. The brushes will come clean more easily. Rinse them in fresh water after washing.

After cleaning a brush in a solvent, wash it in detergent and water if you will not need it again the next day. The bristles will be cleaner and softer. Form them in shape, and hang the brush by its handle to dry at least 24 hours before it is stored away.

Or you can use one of the brush renewers, emulsions or solvents with wetting agents that dissolve oil paints yet allow rinsing with water. You soak the brush in the solution, then flush out any residue of paint under the faucet.

If you are short of cans for cleaning the brushes, use a cardboard milk or cottage cheese carton.

To keep an uncleaned brush soft overnight, just slip it into a plastic food bag and seal by twisting the neck of the bag around the brush handle and securing with a rubber band.

A squirt of the new brush protector that comes in spray cans or a dab into a can of jelly-type brush protector will also keep a brush soft overnight. If you coat the uncleaned brush well with the spray or jelly protector and seal it in a plastic food bag, it should stay soft for weeks.

Cleaning a Roller

First roll it over several sheets of newspaper to remove all the paint you can. Then place it in a mason jar or tall narrow can with a lid, and add some solvent or sudsy water (whichever is required). Then shake it like a cocktail; after renewing the cleaner, shake again. Fluff out the cleaned roller and let stand vertically while it dries. Store it vertically so it will not flatten on one side.

Cleaning Your Hands

To clean stubborn paint spots from your hands, wet a little sawdust with thinner and scrub with it. Or pour a spoonful of powdered borax-base soap in the palm of one hand, wet it with thinner, wash with this, then rinse with water. Your hands will be oily. Wash again with just the soap and water and they will be very clean.

Storing and Re-using Paint

Float a thin layer of paint thinner on top when you put away a can of solvent-thinned paint. This will minimize the "skin" that forms. At the same time, mark the level of the paint on the outside of the can. Later you'll know at a glance if there is enough paint in it for a given job.

When you next use the paint, don't shake the can. Cut the skin around the edge and lift it out with a stirring wand. If the skin breaks up, strain the paint through a nylon stocking (the best disposable strainer for any paint). Also strain latex paint before re-using it, to separate out dried particles. Add only a small amount of water if it seems to need some thinning.

PHOTOGRAPHERS

Cover photograph by **Morley Baer**. **William Aplin:** pages 57, 61. **Jerry Bragstad:** pages 88, 115 (bottom right). **Ernest Braun:** pages 10, 11, 21, 34 (bottom), 35, 36 (left, bottom right), 78 (top, center left, right, bottom left), 79, 90 (bottom), 91, 92. **William Carter:** page 31 (bottom). **Glenn Christiansen:** pages 29, 38, 39, 42, 43 (bottom left), 81 (center right). **Dearborn-Massar:** pages 12, 13, 66 (bottom), 67. **Richard Fish:** pages 18, 19, 20 (bottom), 22, 23, 30, 48 (bottom), 49, 55 (center, bottom left, right), 56 (bottom), 58, 59, 64, 65, 68, 69, 76, 77 (top, bottom right), 94, 95, 100, 101, 102, 104, 105, 106, 107, 108. **Donn Foreman:** page 8 (top). **Joshua Freiwald:** pages 86, 86. **Herrington-Olson Photography:** page 113 (bottom right). **Glen Hunt:** pages 50 (top), 70 (top left). **Roy Krell:** page 53 (bottom right). **Leland Y. Lee:** pages 24, 25. **G. H. Machette:** page 60 (top). **Don Normark:** pages 7 (bottom), 8 (bottom), 9, 14, 15, 16, 17, 26, 28, 32 (bottom left, right), 33, 37, 45 (top left, right), 47 (bottom, 50 (bottom), 51, 71 (bottom), 72, 73, 80, 82 (bottom), 83, 84, 85, 89 (bottom), 93, 115 (top right). **Ray Piper:** page 54 (center, bottom). **Ricco-Mazzuchi Photography:** page 43 (top, bottom right). **Karl H. Riek:** pages 74 (bottom), 75. **Martha Rosman:** pages 27 (top left), 46, 60 (bottom), 115 (top left). **Adrian Saxe:** page 98. **Julius Shulman:** pages 99 (bottom), 103, 115 (bottom left). **Darrow M. Watt:** pages 27 (right), 36 (top right), 40, 41, 44, 78 (bottom right), 96 (left, bottom right), 97, 113 (top, bottom left). **Ray O. Welch:** page 70 (top right, bottom). **Elton Welke:** pages 52, 53 (top, bottom left). **R. Wenkam:** pages 62, 63. **George Woo:** page 81 (bottom).

Sketch renditions on pages 111 and 125 courtesy of Armstrong Cork Company.